Cambridge

M000112310

Elements in Music Since 1945
edited by
Mervyn Cooke
University of Nottingham

HEINER GOEBBELS AND CURATORIAL COMPOSING AFTER CAGE

From Staging Works to Musicalising Encounters

Ed McKeon
Goldsmiths, University of London

CAMBRIDGE
UNIVERSITY PRESS

CAMBRIDGE
UNIVERSITY PRESS

Shaftesbury Road, Cambridge CB2 8EA, United Kingdom

One Liberty Plaza, 20th Floor, New York, NY 10006, USA

477 Williamstown Road, Port Melbourne, VIC 3207, Australia

314–321, 3rd Floor, Plot 3, Splendor Forum, Jasola District Centre, New Delhi – 110025, India

103 Penang Road, #05–06/07, Visioncrest Commercial, Singapore 238467

Cambridge University Press is part of Cambridge University Press & Assessment, a department of the University of Cambridge.

We share the University's mission to contribute to society through the pursuit of education, learning and research at the highest international levels of excellence.

www.cambridge.org
Information on this title: www.cambridge.org/9781009337601

DOI: 10.1017/9781009337618

First published 2022

A catalogue record for this publication is available from the British Library.

ISBN 978-1-009-33760-1 Paperback
ISSN 2632-7791 (online)
ISSN 2632-7783 (print)

Heiner Goebbels and Curatorial Composing after Cage

From Staging Works to Musicalising Encounters

Elements in Music Since 1945

DOI: 10.1017/9781009337618
First published online: October 2022

Ed McKeon
Goldsmiths, University of London
Author for correspondence: Ed McKeon, ed.mckeon@thirdear.co.uk

Abstract: This Element introduces the notion of curatorial composing to account for certain musical practices that emerged from the 1960s as the founding concepts of music as an art – instituted in the modern era – were systematically dismantled. It raises the key question of how musical value and authority might be produced without recourse to an external principle, origin, transcendental framework, or other foundation. It argues that these practices do not dismiss the issue of value or simply relativise it but shift the paradigm to a curatorial concern for composing public encounters and staging events. This Element shows that Lydia Goehr's elaboration of the work-concept provides a framework that was transformed by John Cage in his work from *0'00"* (1962) onwards. The Element then introduces Heiner Goebbels' practice and focuses on his role as Artistic Director of the Ruhrtriennale (2012–14), which it argues was an extension of his curatorial composing.

This Element also has a video abstract: www.cambridge.org/
Music Since 1945_McKeon_abstract
Keywords: work-concept, curatorial, Heiner Goebbels, John Cage, musicality

ISBNs: 9781009337601 (PB), 9781009337618 (OC)
ISSNs: 2632-7791 (online), 2632-7783 (print)

Contents

1 Musical Elements

Anyone who only understands music, doesn't understand that either. Hanns Eisler
(Goebbels, 2015: 73)

I don't think that music should have a definition. That would keep it from being what it necessarily is. *John Cage (2016: 484)*

An elementary particle is not an independent analyzable entity, a basic building block of matter, but rather a set of relationships extending outward to other things. *Natalie Crohn Schmitt (1990: 34)*

This Element touches on elementary questions. Questions of first principles are usually 'the basics' that all can agree on, a preliminary consent on common sense and core concepts that make a shared discourse possible. Introduced to 'beginners', they pave the way for more 'advanced' study. Elementary matters act as keystones on which disciplinary edifices are built.

Looking back from 2022, perhaps the defining characteristic of 'music since 1945' is a *loss of definition* – a loss of foundational certainty – catalysing numerous returns to basics. As composers and artists challenged music's 'first principles', demonstrating that the discipline was not natural or self-evident but constructed, musicologists similarly began to dismantle cherished assumptions of the discipline in earlier repertoires. Elementary questions arose. Is music different from sound, and if so, in what ways? Is all music of equal value or do some forms merit greater consideration, prestige, attention, and study than others? Can music be understood separately from its social, political, and economic contexts? Indeed, can music be understood at all if abstracted from the particular time, place, and circumstances of its experience?

The humbling figure most associated with this return to music's elements is John Cage. I will begin with Cage not in order to put the elements back in place, but to consider with him the specifically *musical* question of what can be done *without* such foundation stones. What becomes possible 'if zero is taken as the basis', as Cage put it, adding 'that's the part that isn't often understood' (Kostelanetz, 1988: 208). Conventional wisdom claims that such gnomic statements came from Cage's turn to Eastern philosophies, especially Zen Buddhism. By contrast, I show that he was following the musical logic of his composition teacher, Arnold Schoenberg, but rejecting the Austrian's definition of music's 'basic unit' (*Grundgestalt*). Without an a priori principle such as 'musical' tones that could be fixed in notational form, the concept of 'music' began to lose definition.

In pursuing the consequences of this move in the work of Heiner Goebbels, I want to underscore a distinction between 'music' and 'the musical' – or 'musicality' – to acknowledge that the latter is not dependent on the former, and that compositional forms can be manifest without sound, in 'non-musical' mediums such as video installations or watercolours, and especially in the construction of encounters.[1] In brief, whilst Cage has been appreciated as a gallery artist and Goebbels as a 'postdramatic' theatre-maker and installation artist, both are composers shaped by musical concerns. The composed relationship of form and content shifts here from the work to the event and resonates in novel ways with invocations of 'the musical' (*das Musikalische*) by Schiller, Schlegel, and others from the late eighteenth century as a key concept both for aesthetics and for philosophical practice more broadly (Bowie, 2007; Goehr, 2017). For now, then, let 'the musical' indicate a structuring process irreducible to any prior principle, definition, origin, or foundation. It is in this sense that the title of this Element in *Music Since 1945* refers to the notion of 'curatorial composing' for the musicalisation of events in which music – conventionally understood – may form only a part.

This approach demands a parallel shift in methodology with significant implications for readers from differing 'subject' positions. It would be perverse either to place such anti-foundational practices within the accepted conventions of an established discipline or to build a narrative 'from the ground up', from elementary conditions. This will not, then, be a musicological study in the customary sense; nor does it fall wholly within sub-disciplinary topics such as concert studies and performance curation – though readers familiar with these literatures will, I expect, find much to engage with. Rather than put a new foundation in place, I aim to draw out a metamorphosis of musical possibilities by putting in counterpoint aspects of music theory, philosophy, (ethno)musicology, and art history.[2]

Musicology has itself been divided at least since the late 1980s by the felt loss of its foundational supports and the value structures they once sustained, torn between considerations of its proper objects of study – whether scores, recordings, or performances – and the social, environmental, political, and economic contexts in which they arise. The fault line of this split falls over another divide, that between aesthetics and ethics. On the one hand, music's objects are invested with value, implicitly or explicitly made significant if not canonic; on the other, contextual studies are usually more concerned with music's role in the articulation of identities and relations within social systems structured by power.

---

[1] By 'encounter' I am pointing to Louis Althusser's *Philosophy of the Encounter* (2006), though Cage's project takes the notion further, as I have argued elsewhere (McKeon, 2021).

[2] My narrative includes elements of participant observation, both as an audience member – in particular of Goebbels' work – and as a curatorial producer of post-experimental music, including staging performances of Cage and events by Goebbels.

Rather than adjudicate by privileging either production or reception, musical object or political reality, I follow the immanent compositional logics of Cage and Goebbels in constructing encounters that address both together through musical form whereby value is *both* aesthetic and ethical.

This partitioning between the work of artists and the contribution of audiences and publics is not limited to musicology, of course. Visual culture studies made thematic the problems of mediating objects and subjects, products of culture and of nature, through the prism of a constitutive visual difference. In contrast with vision as a physiological apparatus, 'visuality' marked the asymmetrical chiasm whereby to know (*savoir*) was already to see (*voir*), but to see was no longer simply to know. Plain sight – like plain thinking – was ideological. Visuality concerned, for example, the work of 'scopic regimes' in producing subjects identifying with and troubled by self-representations: in a world constituted by identity and difference, the subject becomes an object for itself and for others.[3] It comes as no surprise that visual culture studies emerged contemporaneously with curatorial studies in the late 1980s, overlapping with theories of visual art *after* painting and sculpture to account for practices that were not predominantly optical.[4] For example, sound art – in similar ways to its sibling sound studies, a younger cousin of visual culture studies – has been conceptualised and differentiated from music through this problematic of mediation. It was either primarily conceptual (or rather, 'postconceptual', the 'condition' of art after Conceptual Art (Osborne, 2018)) and so in contrast with music's supposed emphasis on the phenomenal experience of sound, or it was vibrational, pre-subjective and pre-conceptual, and so again unlike music now conceived as already constituted by conceptually entrained modes of listening. Within the gallery, in short, curating has been preoccupied with 'ocularcentrism', the myopia of visual knowledge, to the exclusion of musical practices and musical logic.

This has come at a cost. The profession has faced continual crises over its proper relations to art and museum history, art theory, techniques of display, artists' social practices, and the formation of observant publics (McKeon, 2021). In particular, attempts to establish a 'critical' visuality have foundered

[3] Rosalind Krauss (1993: 14) summarised (and diagrammed) this most succinctly: '*Figure* versus *ground*, then. The fundamentals of perception. The opposition without which no vision at all: vision occurring precisely in the dimension of difference, of separation, of bounded objects emerging as apart from, in contrast to, the ambiance or ground within which they appear.'
[4] At the time of founding the first course in Critical and Curatorial Studies in 1987 at the Whitney Independent Study Program, Hal Foster (1988) was also convening and publishing proceedings from a discussion on 'Vision and Visuality'. Indeed, Martin Jay – whose *Downcast Eyes* (1993) provided one of the most substantial accounts of visual critique – later argued that 'in hindsight, *Vision and Visuality* may be seen as the moment when the visual turn … really showed signs of turning into the academic juggernaut it was to become in the 1990s' (Jay, 2002: 267).

on the paradox of trying to correct the poverty of 'pure vision' with a more discerning 'eye', or a perspective capable of staring at its own optical distortions. Similar difficulties, I suggest, occur with attempts to apply the discourse of critical curating to contemporary music, which focus predominantly on the politics and ethics of selection or programming, as if a more receptive ear might compensate for the erosion of any essential distinction marking out one musical heritage from our field of seemingly limitless possibilities. Rendered as a form of judicious selection, the notion of curating left the museum's hallowed confines to become almost ubiquitous (Balzer, 2015). Music playlists, restaurant menus, data gathering, and the production of festivals and other myriad experiences are now routinely 'curated'. As a result, many of its practitioners in the formerly 'visual' arts have abandoned the term. More significantly for my purposes, some theorists of the discipline have proffered 'the curatorial' – an adjectival noun, like 'the musical' – as a conceptual gambit with which to address directly the problem of mediation and to do so without privileging the visual, critical or otherwise; indeed, without imposing any elementary or founding framework (Martinon, 2013). The curatorial is premised neither on the task of 'making visible' nor on 'revealing' an inner, hidden, or invisible truth. For at least one prominent theorist, this too has shifted the question of value from one predominantly concerned with aesthetics and art theory to one equally understood as a practice of ethics (Martinon, 2021). Curatorial composing complements this approach.

One influential elaboration of the construction of music's foundation in its modern form – 'classical' and beyond – and its erosion in more recent times is presented through the 'musical work-concept', as developed philosophically and critiqued by Lydia Goehr in *The Imaginary Museum of Musical Works* (2007). I will proceed with a schematic reading of her argument, in part as her title suggestively implies the 'imaginary' work of the curator and in part as she deliberates at length on the limits of this elementary condition in the work of John Cage, especially on *4'33"* (1952), his 'silent' piece. In contrast with Goehr, I will show how Cage dislodged this keystone in particular in his later practice from *0'00"* (1962) – or *4'33" No.2*, as he dubbed it – which marked a turn towards the social articulation of staging encounters. Placing this within the context of his studies with Schoenberg and his later turn towards other media – including texts, typography, printmaking, and watercolours – I show how his compositional logic was manifest in such curatorial projects as his *Musicircus* and *museumcircle*.

Having established this example of curatorial composing, I turn to Heiner Goebbels. I show how his practice similarly moves beyond any notion of 'music itself' and argue that his technique of sampling can be understood as a compositional principle that could be 'scaled up' from a snippet of recorded music or sound through to whole productions presented whilst Artistic Director of the Ruhrtriennale (2012–14). Just as strategies of appropriation render moot the question of originality so, I claim, Goebbels shifts the issue of authorship. I develop this with a focus on his astonishing production of Louis Andriessen's *De Materie* (2014), and in particular on an otherworldly scene marking the transition into its fourth movement. This then provides a point of reference through which I examine other dimensions of his practice: his composition of temporal and spatial relations; his consideration of the public and the situation of encounter; and his overriding concern for the signifying affect of wonder that animates this.

The work of Hannah Arendt and Elias Canetti – both inspirations for Goebbels – guide my approach, to which I add that of the philosopher Catherine Malabou. I will show that his interest lies less in appropriation as such and more with the polyphonic staging of public encounters in which each element – lighting, scenography, text, performers, sound design, and music – features as an independent 'voice' in counterpoint with others. This form of composition is designed to shift the relationship between audience and perform- ance from one of an implicit detached listening and observation to a situation akin to what Arendt called a 'space of appearance' in which value is articulated as a mode of public encounter.

2 The Work-Concept and Its Limits

In order to appreciate the notion of curatorial composing, it helps first to detach the notion of composing from the concept of the 'musical work'. Curatorial practice here is not something that acts on works by making them public. Rather, it is the composing itself of the elements of an encounter. I begin by briefly developing the musical work-concept as elaborated by Lydia Goehr, which I approach schematically and synoptically in a manner distinct from her own method. This will both clarify her presentation of Cage's *4'33"* as a limit point that does not dispense with but rather reinforces the notion of a musical work and will provide a framework with which to return with Cage to question whether his late work really does leave this foundational structure intact.

The work-concept is fundamentally a question of musical value – or more precisely, of musical authority. Goehr's *Imaginary Museum* first appeared in 1992, precisely at the time that the New Musicology was dismantling the idealist trappings of the Western classical canon and its concert practices, and also just as curatorial studies emerged in recognition of the problematic stature that curators had acquired. It marked a moment when modernist notions of musical value and its prestige were being deconstructed and when a new and disconcertingly performative form of value production – the power to make visible – was being established. Her work has often been celebrated by those welcoming the elimination of Western classical music's privileged status, but this has frequently obscured her ongoing concern for the production of aesthetic value, a concern that by no means abandons the work-concept. I will follow her critique and its implications for musical aesthetics in turn.

Goehr does not set out to define what a musical work is. Rather, she addresses the question of definition itself as an historical project, a consequential project that structured classical music as a set of cultural practices. A notion of music was needed 'around 1800', she claims, to give it a value that would dignify the work of composers and musicians alongside their counterparts in the literary and 'fine arts'. Within the emerging field of philosophical aesthetics, especially in the writings of Kant and Hegel, music ranked the lowest of the arts. It was considered too emotional and subjective to ground an objective appreciation of beauty. In the case of instrumental music, detached from language and discourse and so lacking a concept, it was too diffuse, ethereal, and ephemeral to offer a revelation of universal truths. In this context, the notion of the musical work – or rather, of *Werktreue*, fidelity to the work's 'inner' truth – provided a kind of philosophical anchor, a foundation stone on which this imaginary museum might be built (Bonds, 2006, 2014).

This idea of an *imaginary* museum, adopted from André Malraux's essay on the 'Museum Without Walls' (1974), helpfully draws attention to a crucial distinction between the work-*concept* and any concrete pieces this structure might contain. The framing concept defines and distinguishes what is and what is not 'music'; works themselves are founded through conventions of author-ship. In describing the musical work as a 'regulative concept', Goehr indicates that it is not only an Ideal category, a fixed and eternal notion of Art determining what can or cannot be viewed or listened to as such. It is instead historically contingent and shifting, and so requires new 'galleries' and shifting strategies of display reflecting contemporary understanding. To acknowledge her borrowing from Wittgenstein, the musical work-concept is an ongoing curatorial 'language game' and task concerning the lawful relationship between artists' constantly innovating practices and the identity or ideal self-image of the field itself.

With this distinction, the question of the work-concept shifts from that of definition – of what a musical work *is* – to what effect it is designed to achieve. In Freudian terms, the work-concept can be understood to function like a homeostatic principle, a means of maintaining a (human) subject's continuity and integrity over time, ever ageing yet always recognisably the same, defending the organism from trauma and avant-gardist 'shocks of the new' by regulating the relationship between its 'outside' and 'inside'. Goehr therefore emphasises two principal tasks that it performs. On the one hand, it is concerned with the production of musical *autonomy*, the distinction between 'music itself' and its social function or context – the '*extra*-musical'. On the other, the work-concept addresses the issue of 'medium specificity', of what makes music 'music' – the question of music's essence.[5]

These are the conditions that structured what has become familiar as Western classical music and its cultural practices. Goehr draws attention to several recognisable characteristics, which I divide here according to my schematic outline of her argument. On the one hand, the construction of public concert halls as dedicated spaces for music performance separate from everyday life helped to constitute music's autonomy with its own hallowed rituals, which in turn necessitated a new type of entrained listening supported by music criticism, programme notes, and the pedagogical project of 'music appreciation'. 'Musical' listening was necessarily differentiated from commonplace hearing (Thorau and Ziemer, 2019). A host of intermediary roles ensued, tasked, for example, with concert production, programming, artist management, and promotion. The public was further distanced from this institutional form of music through the distinction of amateur and professional, with repertoire for the latter gaining in complexity and virtuosity and so requiring specialisation and elevation in ways that paralleled a division between the tastes of connoisseurs and the broader public.

On the other hand, musical works were articulated as exemplars of music's essence through an increasing separation of composers – who acquired what Foucault (1998) called the 'author function' – from performers. This placed an emphasis on the definitive score (or *Urtext*) as a true original that was both permanent and perfectly repeatable, distinct from improvised forms and practices of transcription, arrangement, musical borrowing or parody, and also differentiated from juvenilia, sketches, and so on. It also required faithful interpretation, with increasing standardisation of notation and performance conventions such as metronome markings and concert tuning in order for works always and everywhere to be played 'correctly', at least in principle. Lastly, works were given an ancestry and lineage – the musical canon – that obscured the work-concept's own historical emergence. For example, Goehr

---

[5] This relationship between autonomy, which regulates an external border, and essence – commonly a transcendental principle – provides the structural logic of a *parergon* as elaborated by Derrida (1987), notably, in visual terms, in relation to painting. As a supplement to the work – the *ergon* – it operates like a passe-partout 'between that which is framed and that which is framing in the frame' (24). It distinguishes inside from outside, whilst also indicating an interior (and anterior) perspective or 'inside of the inside'.

argued that J. S. Bach did not write works because the work-concept was not operative when he composed, yet his music acquired the ontological status of works through a retrospective gaze (Steingo, 2014). Her claim that 'it is rather a contingent, retroactively discovered, bonding and roping process' (Goehr, 2007: 108) thus echoed Malraux's statement that 'the notion of art as such must first come into being, if the past is to acquire an artistic value' (Malraux, 1974: 53). It also resonates with Arendt's argument in her essay 'What Is Authority?' (1961), an issue that runs through Heiner Goebbels' work and to which I will return.

The work-concept's operation on music history was matched by its attention to contemporary practices. Goehr does not develop an historical account of this process but dwells on what she perceives to be its continuing utility *after* the erasure and erosion of many of the cultural practices through which it had taken regulative form.

> I was interested in how persons thought in the past to increase understanding of how we think in the present under the regulation of the work-concept, even though the reason I wanted to understand how we think in the present was to prevent our concluding that this is the only way to think (Goehr, 2007: xliv).

More specifically, she is concerned precisely with the question of authority in the wake of the work-concept's decline. In contrast with what I characterised as the turn to ethical considerations by many writers in the New Musicology, her focus remains consistently on aesthetics. The challenge was to avoid either the work-concept's continuing operation by fiat or its uncritical application (or relativisation) to other music practices. 'The generic work-concept apparently stripped of all historical meaning or the view of a row of perspectives equalized and standardized: these are both positions upon which some of the most dangerous forms of modern authority have come to depend' (Goehr, 2007: xlv).[6] In short, with the weakening of the work-concept – of the articulation of Western classical music's foundations – the question of aesthetic value had neither been nullified nor made arbitrary but remained a productive problematic and task.

On the one hand, the extension of the concept to jazz, folk, and film music could be understood as adapting its force, not abolishing it. Marking a relation of 'derivative' to 'original' use of the work-concept, this approach could lead to its refinement and evolution. On the other hand, Goehr argues, attempts to contest the work-concept from 'within the musical institution' are doomed to

---

[6] The persistence of this binary can be seen, for example, in the arguments advanced by Boris Johnson's former adviser Munira Mirza (2012), endorsing claims for transcendental 'universalism' – an unquestionable essence of art – as the premise for and counterpart to the sovereign individual in opposition to 'relativist' arguments for cultural diversity. As has often been noted, this privileges some individuals as more sovereign than others.

failure for two reasons: 'First, those who wish to challenge a concept's regulative force usually find themselves paradoxically situated in a practice that is regulated by the very concept they want to challenge; second, that a regulative concept's alteration or demise is no less complicated a process than its emergence.' (Goehr, 2007: 260)

Cage's music – and *4′33″* in particular – provides her exemplar. To begin with, she argues that by accepting the terms of concert practice by which its authority was exercised, the framework of *Werktreue* had actually been consolidated. Its silences may have shocked in the 1950s, but the celebrated composer's eccentricities had been absorbed with benign good humour by the 1990s; its score continues to be performed to appreciative audiences. Cage maintained his promise to Schoenberg, she noted, as a composer of musical works, however far he may have stretched the term. The historical lesson of this structural problematic came from the fate of the avant-garde – as outlined by Peter Bürger (1984) – whereby the 'anti-art' of Dada, the Futurists, and Constructivists was soon incorporated into museum and private collections, the objects of curators' recuperative projects to reconfigure art history. Cage may have weakened the discourse of music's essence, the work-concept's 'internal' articulation, but its external border – its separation from the everyday – remained firmly secure.

I will focus on *0′00″* to show how Cage began to break this framework down further, but the critique of his musical silence merits a brief reflection. For example, Richard Taruskin attacked Cage in typically pugilistic fashion, writing to bury his legacy shortly after the composer's death:

> Sounds that were noise on one side of an arbitrary framing gesture are suddenly music, a 'work of art', on the other side; the esthetic comes into being by sheer fiat . . . .. The audience is invited – no, commanded – to listen to ambient or natural sounds with the same reverent contemplation they would assume if they were listening to Beethoven's Ninth. (Taruskin, 2009: 275)

To claim that *4′33″* *commands* silent listening because of its *un*-notated performance conventions is both a misrepresentation of any actual performance – it famously provokes giggles, coughing, and audible nervous twitching in concert halls – and a projective 'reading' of its instructions and intent. Goehr is more measured, stating only that it remains within the work-concept 'because of his specifications that people gather together, usually in a concert hall, to listen to the sounds of the hall for the allotted time period'. Yet the various scored versions of *4′33″* make no such specifications.[7] Moreover, the premiere, at Woodstock, was given in the Maverick Concert Hall, the back doors of whose barn-like structure were opened to the surrounding rural environment, whilst the

---

[7] On the different versions of the score, see Gann (2010: chapter 5).

most famous document of Cage's own performance – in Nam June Paik's 1974 documentary *Tribute to John Cage* – took place in Harvard Square surrounded by students, passers-by, and traffic.

Goehr would no doubt also disagree with Taruskin's characterisation of the framing aesthetic discourse as 'arbitrary'. On the contrary, she argues that such a framing gesture remained a necessity. The determination of what is or is not an artistic work was not merely a conceit of power but constantly negotiated, and it was this process that constituted the value of the work-concept. Whilst the 'locus' of music's authority was now in doubt – potentially to be reclaimed 'in the work itself, in its realization through performance, or in the interpretive act of listening to a work' (275) – the positing of the question itself remains unavoidable. Any new consensus would, as before, depend on the language games of 'complex theories, and the practices to which these theories become attached'. In this minimal sense of preserving musical art's autonomy from the social everyday – or 'the commonplace', as Arthur Danto (1981) put it – the work-concept remains operational. 'Sounds that were noise on one side' of the frame might indeed become 'suddenly music' on the other, but what matters is the 'fidelity' to a conception of how this might be achieved. The transfigur-ation of the 'extra-musical' into the musical corpus requires the work of theory, and for Goehr this applies as much to Cage's *4′33″* as to any other musical work.

Returning to these issues in *Elective Affinities* (2008), Goehr elaborates the possibilities for changing the paradigm once more in relation to Cage's musical silence, considering it alongside Max Neuhaus' *Times Square* (1977–92), a concealed sound installation in the New York district that blended almost seamlessly with the surrounding acoustic environment. Cage's work was expli-cit in exposing the work-concept's limits, she argues, but did so from within the institution; Neuhaus' critique was implicit and therefore perhaps 'more subver-sive', whilst the artist nevertheless claimed his work to be a work. 'The question here is whether it is more effective to challenge the work-concept from the outside or from the inside, by an external and explicit idea or by changing conditions that internally compel a change in our understanding' (Goehr, 2008: 85). Siding with Adorno and Danto, her exemplars for theorising contemporary music and art, she opts for the latter. Our understanding 'can only be developed by reflecting historically from inside the musical experience itself'. This logic – that the work-concept could only be reconfigured immanently and dialectically through its internal contradictions – is correct, I argue, but the understanding of Cage on which it is developed is not. He did not fail because he attempted to impose 'external' ideas – from Zen Buddhism, for example – on musical practice whilst firmly established 'within' music's institutions. The shift from composing works to composing encounters – to curatorial composing – involves precisely an immanent transformation of the field, which is why it is essential to appreciate Cage's practice through his studies with Schoenberg.

Before attending to this, a quick summary will help. I have outlined Goehr's position in some detail because it poses the dual questions of music's autonomy and essence side by side, and it does so specifically in relation to Cage as a key figure in the destabilisation of both. The work-concept articulated music as a subject, providing continuity over time, defined by its interiority and the relation to its exterior social and acoustic environment. The former – music's foundational identity – was mutable, open to being located in the work, the performance, or the listener; the latter – music's autonomy – remained unbroken, marking a distinction between quotidian and artistic experiences. The paradigm shift that I am arguing for, signalled by Cage's late work, therefore involves not simply composing events as if they are works, but a reconfiguration of music's 'internal' and 'external' relations, its essence and autonomy, as constitutive of claims to musical value.

3 Variable Time: Cage after Schoenberg

I believe . . . that it is primarily because of [Cage's] music – his very substantial credibility as a composer – that we are drawn into a consideration of his philosophical and theoretical ideas. *James Tenney (1983/2015: 283)*

As Goehr noted, Cage often emphasised the importance of his studies with Schoenberg (ca.1935–7). Whilst the impact of this experience for Cage was questioned in the 1990s (Hicks, 1990; Parsons Smith, 1995), its significance – primarily for his earlier work – is now more widely accepted (Bernstein, 2002; Ravenscroft, 2006; Neff, 2014). I aim to show that the logic of Schoenberg's method provided a model that he was able to adapt, and that understood in these terms can be grasped as an evolving project into his later practice. Where influence has been traced, it remains attached to his more-or-less conventionally scored pieces of the 1940s and 1950s; my concern is for how it opened the possibility of practising in forms not understood as 'music' – such as printmaking, watercolours, video installations, and the composing of encounters. In short, this immanent move marks a shift from music to musicality.

Schoenberg insisted fundamentally on music as an immanent and dialectical form. The imposition of preformed and transcendental aesthetic ideas to contain it was inadequate. Thus, for example, 'Beauty, an undefined concept, [was] quite useless as a basis for aesthetic discrimination' (Schoenberg, 1983: 195). The distinction between music and not-music was not determined by an 'arbitrary frame' distinguishing an inside and outside of musical art, but an historically necessary and internally motivated logic, a critical development pursued dialectically between continuity and innovation (Schoenberg, 1948/1975; Cherlin, 2000). Writing a year after Cage's studies with him, he emphasised that 'one cannot really understand the style of one's time if one has not found out how it is distinguished from the style of one's predecessors' (Schoenberg, 1938/1975: 377). Musical and historical movement came from comprehending the contradictions inherent in a given order as they appear to an unfolding and emergent potentiality. Change came neither from 'outside', imposed as an abstraction, nor merely as an accident of history, but as a self-reflexive movement specific to music's own technical and material present. It was through the dialectical tension between the socially situated composer's subjective freedom ('anything goes', as Cage put it) and the objective necessity in the limits imposed by music's historical development ('but not everything is attempted', he added (Cage, 1954/1968: 160)) that the question of aesthetic value played out: 'It receives its legitimacy from the tradition it negates' (Adorno, 1992: 155).

For Schoenberg, this meant accepting the logical consequences of Wagnerian harmony for musical form. The late eighteenth-century tonal system of keys had offered a musical syntax based on the dominance of 'centripetal' functions – of harmonic movement from and directed back towards the 'endings' of cadential closure – over 'centrifugal' tendencies that explored more remote harmonic 'regions' that offered greater expressive variety. Romantic composers had increasingly pushed beyond the gravitational pull of tonal centres and their relational orbits. The 'vertical' harmonic field was increasingly stretched into the horizontal as an instant projected towards the infinite.[8] Traditional musical forms could barely contain the harmonic implications of this material; as a result, the duration of works increased substantially. Dissonance needed to be 'emancipated', then, because it was no longer to be defined by consonance and the closure it provided. Music's formal necessity of 'logic and coherence', its identity of form and content, therefore had to be achieved organically by generating all of a work's material – its thematic and harmonic 'content', its horizontal and vertical dimensions, respectively – from the same motivic *idea* (element or seed). This was his celebrated notion of the *Grundgestalt*, the 'basic shape' from which a work's form would be self-generating (Schoenberg, 1931/1975: 289).

---

[8] This temporal affect – or feeling of time, particularly to a certain *fin-de-siècle* European historicity – was precisely expressed by Schoenberg in describing his intention with *Erwartung* (1909), a work that marked his decisive shift beyond tonal logic, 'to represent in slow motion everything that occurs during a single second of maximum spiritual excitement, stretching it out to half an hour' (Schoenberg, 1975: 105).

Crucially, in order to avoid creating unintended harmonic expectations by accidentally reinstating distinctions of consonance and dissonance, or negating the formal dialectical principle of irreversible change by use of unvaried repetition, a rigorous and disciplined method was needed to maintain their equilibrium (Schoenberg, 1975: 102–4). Adorno (1998) summarised the issue as follows:

> As a developmental structure music is an absolute negation of repetition, in accordance with Heraclitus' assertion that no one ever steps into the same river twice. On the other hand, it is only able to develop by virtue of repetition. Thematic work, the principle which concretizes the abstract passage of time in terms of musical substance, is never more than the dissimilarity of the similar. (284)

The contrapuntal procedure of *developing variation* – derived from Brahms – provided just such an approach. Here, a single musical 'idea' generated a limited set of possibilities – configurations in two-dimensional (vertical and horizontal) musical 'space' – that could be set in motion without repetition to generate form by controlling the number of *variables* (like 'a Diophantine equation'). This was a music *embodying* historical movement as a dialectical process, each variation both derived from the music before it and generative for what followed, and its logic was fundamental to Cage's studies with Schoenberg (Cage, 2016: 20, 22).

Whilst suspending systematically the temporal logic of consonance and dissonance, Schoenberg had nevertheless accepted the historical convention of the twelve-note tempered scale as a limitation, a principle he consolidated (and reified) with dodecaphonic serialism as a method determined by the permutational possibilities of their sequential ordering. Indeed, as Adorno pointed out, this latter move had not only betrayed his musical dialectics by imposing from 'outside' an arbitrary structural frame; the traditional musical forms that Schoenberg continued to employ no longer functioned according to their earlier principles of harmonic tension and release. In short, form and content were not identical. The relation of music's vertical and horizontal dimensions needed to be transformed, and so musical time rethought: 'each tone and each instant should be equally near the centre, and this would preclude the organization of musical time progression which prevails in Schoenberg' (Adorno, 1992: 161, 1998: 271, 286). Rhythm and timbre (sonority or 'tone colours', distinct sonic qualities produced by different instruments) now took on greater significance. 'Of all of Schoenberg's accomplishments in integrating musical means, not the least was that he conclusively separated color from the decorative sphere and elevated it to a compositional element in its own right'.

Cage's next step has to be understood in this context if we are to grasp the significance of his *methodical* introduction of chance operations into his compositions. It is precisely this that Adorno missed in his critique; indeed, what is immediately striking about his analysis is just how closely this describes key aspects of Cage's music in the 1950s. His departures from this programme should then be understood not as an abandonment of tradition but as its further dialectical sublation.[9]

Cage famously had 'no sense of harmony'. In his early work, he rejected as an arbitrary constraint the principle of octave equivalence – the tempered scale and its twelve-step division – that Schoenberg had himself extensively analysed. In contrast to the residual idealism of Adorno, this meant *letting go of the precondition* of 'musical' tones, which Adorno regarded as fundamentally necessary for establishing pitch relations as the basis for musical dialectics.

> The site of all musicality is a priori an interior space and only here does it become constituted as an objective reality. .... In it the external objectivity returns as the objectivity of the subject itself. (Adorno, 1998: 300)

Two-dimensional pitch space was foundational of musical time. One note alone lacked the principle of relation from which music's temporal form was created, he argued (implicitly critiquing composers such as Giacinto Scelsi), whilst composers' turns to instrumental colour and tone quality as a structural parameter was an imported abstraction (a bassoon has no immanent relation to a violin or a gong). 'Sound and music diverge' (301).[10]

> Through its autonomy the sound regains a culinary quality which is irreconcilable with the constructive principle. The density of material and colour has done nothing to modify the dissociative character of the structure, which remains external. Dynamism remains [an] elusive ... goal. (313)

---

[9] Goehr (2008: chapter 1) emphasises – following Adorno – that the dialectical principle at play in developing variation was also true for philosophical dialectics itself, a point echoed for example in Frederic Jameson's *The Hegel Variations* (2010). Similar arguments are developed by Andrew Bowie in his *Philosophical Variations* (2010) and *Music, Philosophy, and Modernity* (2007). The dialectical sublation I refer to here can likewise be approached in terms of philosophy with Catherine Malabou's *The Future of Hegel* (2005). That is, the relation of Cage to Schoenberg can be understood as structurally analogous to what Malabou considers dialectics after dialectics, or the gesture of returning to Hegel *after* Hegelianism from which she recuperates the morphological notion of *plasticity*.

[10] Drawing on Hegel and a tradition of musical thought going back at least to Francis Bacon, Hanslick similarly had emphasised that only 'The sound of humanly produced tones ... creates forms that move through time' (Bonds, 2014: 147).

Whilst following in the wake of other composers who explored sounds and noises rather than musical tones – notably Henry Cowell, but also Luigi Russolo, Edgard Varèse, and others writing for non-pitched percussion – Cage's distinctive and primary concern was to adapt and further develop Schoenberg's variation principle by allowing each sound to come from its own centre without being determined by its relation to those around it. 'Harmony' was, in fact, already a function of the temporal gap between perception and cognition: the time it takes to hear is *shorter* than the time it takes to understand or recognise a sound, to process it conceptually and render it 'musical'. As James Tenney (1983/2015) observed, each sound emerges through and as temporal difference due to the cultured mechanisms of listening and its *Gestalt* functions – a distinguishing feature of music, for Cage, from the visual arts.[11] Perception and cognition have their own musical rhythm; sound's immediacy was not already mediated. Three-dimensional 'sound-space' of the listening situation displaced the two-dimensional 'harmonic space' of the musical object. His preliminary revolution, then, was to turn from a system in which musical time was a function of harmony towards a situation where harmony became a function of musical time.

After turning to percussion and other untuned instruments for generating sounds, Cage's adoption of chance techniques provided a systematic means to organise relations between form and content: to produce continual variety *without* a germinal idea. That is, in place of a musical 'idea' – a theme and its motivic potential – as the generative motor or foundation of a composition, Cage left a void but retained the *morphological* principle of constant change. This composition of musical time undergoing differential alteration was a function of the listening experience such that the play of memory and expectation would not reproduce the feeling of temporal continuity of a self that remained essentially unchanged, always the same. Sounds punctuate time, here, but listening articulates it. The self is not apart from but a part of the change experienced (Cage, 1973: 3; Crohn Schmitt, 1990: 8–16).

Now conceived as a temporal model in which variables were controlled to avoid producing relations of dependency with their own expectations, this principle of variation was at first balanced by and contained in 'empty vessels', pre-fixed durational structures that could accept diverse sounds (which Cage called 'gamuts' – aggregates or assortments, without order) such that each

---

[11] That Cage may have consciously drawn on such an extended notion of harmony is shown in his letter to Peter Yates, 14 December 1940: 'I have searched . . . for what characterizes an art, what it is an art is doing that's different from another art. It seems to me that music is very close to the nervous system . . . .The way I've put it in the past is that it's irritating if you can't use it, and pleasing if you can. Whereas things you look at either interest you or don't' (Cage, 2016: 49).

would marvel in its own splendour. 'It is like an empty glass into which at any moment anything may be poured', he claimed in his 1949 'Lecture on Nothing' (Cage, 1968: 109–127), which is why he could perform its wry paradox: 'I have nothing to say and I am saying it'.

Scandalising the European avant-garde at Darmstadt in 1958 – and as a riposte to an article by his former ally Pierre Boulez on 'Chance' ('Alea', (Boulez, 1986)), which denounced its dicey 'intellectual devilry' by 'humble frauds' – Cage gave three lectures ('Composition as Process' (Cage, 1968: 18–56)) that demonstrated the rigorous approach he took to refining this technique. His work had changed. By introducing unknowns into his compositional method using chance operations – beginning with *Music of Changes* (1951) – to avoid relational dependencies, he had gradually been able to dispense with the structural scaffolding of his pre-fabricated (static) structures.[12] Musical time then became a function solely of the developing variation technique of form, 'the morphology of a continuity'.

The laborious and elaborate processes undertaken to achieve this are detailed by James Pritchett (1993) and in Cage's correspondence with Boulez from the early 1950s (Nattiez, 1994: 105–7), but an important aspect of his compositional *discipline* has been overlooked. In searching for complex forms that might 'imitate nature in the manner of her operation' whilst evading synthesis according to entrained concepts of listening, Cage discovered that complexity emerged with the introduction of *five* variables. Five elements complicate the differential logic of the square of oppositions (A, B, not-A, not-B); it was the fifth harmonic (5:4) that destabilised the Pythagorean modelling of the twelve-note scale (Heller-Roazen, 2011); and only from five did the number of binary permutations exceed the number of variables by double or more (Cage, 1968: 173, 1981a: 93, n.2, second interview; Retallack, 1996: 237–8, 297, 344). Giving further variables over to chance techniques – notably the five sound qualities of frequency (pitch), amplitude (loudness), duration, timbre, and order of succession – as with *Variations I* (1958), enabled sounds to become simply 'events in a field of possibilities'.

It is imperative to understand that in stripping away his personal taste, aspects of compositional control, and cultural convention, this was *not* a process of

---

[12] Whilst Cage specified durations in later works, notably the 'number pieces', this was a radically different procedure. Durational units were not structural determinants, as in his earlier work, but *variable* structures, a technique for inviting virtuoso musicians to risk the specific timing of musical events as gestures that were both necessary and non-intentioned, never quite capable of controlled articulation, on the edge of playability. Somewhat akin to his works using cactus plants and conch shells (*Child of Tree*, *Inlets*), sounds were specified but unpredictable, making of their performance not a demonstration of mastery – of virtuosity – but a public manifestation of devotion and *virtue* (Retallack, 1996: 246–90; Riley, 2021: 113–15).

erasure indifferent to the sounding result. Quite the opposite. It was a controlled means for organising the interdependencies of variables such that no one element would be in a hierarchical or determining relation with another, thereby allowing a temporal movement of constant and continuous transformation. Whilst critics such as Perloff (2012) have interpreted this as a flaw or contradiction in Cage's aesthetic, not a renunciation but rather the return of his disavowed ego, they miss the significance of his method. Discipline is required to forego the critical detachment that separates the self from experience.[13] In terms of listening, sheer randomness is like a lottery prone to the (mis)fortunes of accidental coincidence and so potentially experienced as meaningful or prophetic – determined by a prior, external, and supposed 'higher order' of authorial intent or divine intervention; by contrast, Cage's deliberate use of chance aimed to nullify such projection of good or ill, allowing each occurrence to occupy its own centre. Anything goes, '*but only when nothing is taken as the basis*'; at the same time, 'Anything goes. *However, not everything is attempted*' (Cage, 1954/1968: 160, 1974/1979: 178).

One of Cage's favourite aphorisms confirms this. Recollecting his studies with Schoenberg, he gave an account of his teacher's practice of giving his class musical problems to solve, problems with several potential solutions. Having offered new solutions until all possibilities were exhausted, Schoenberg then demanded the common principle underlying all of them. Speechless, Cage regarded him with awe. Only later in the 1970s did he propose an answer; the underlying principle was the question asked (Cage, 1968: 93, 1983: 131–2, 2016: 441, 466).[14] He even presented this in the form of a mesostic - itself a visual and typographical model of the principle - in 'Composition in Retrospect' (Figure 1). Asked about the 'shape' of his Norton Lectures at Harvard (1988–9), he replied: 'a set of variations and the theme is not given'.

In dispensing with pre-fixed durational structures, Cage's music no longer had 'beginnings, middles, and endings'. They were, rather, 'occasions for

---

[13] Related criticisms are made of Cage's apparently naïve belief in the possibility of accessing 'natural' experience, as if the separation of culture from nature can be overcome. For Cage, however, just as intention and non-intention are not opposites, so culture and nature are also intertwined dialectically without a hard distinction or the subsumption of one by the other (Crohn Schmitt, 1990: 16–18).

[14] This was the method for 'polymorphous canon' and 'polymorphous texture' described by Schoenberg in 'Linear Counterpoint' (1931/1975), whereby 'point and opposing point are placed as if right and left of the "equals" sign, hinting at many possible solutions, or sound combinations'. Situating variables as functions of each other's morphology – as if either side of the 'equals' sign – is precisely the approach Cage describes in his Darmstadt lectures. As he explained to Joan Retallack (1996: 63–4) in one of his last interviews: 'I try in general to use chance operations – each number that I use, I try to have it do one thing rather than two things. . . . I try to get an event divided into all the different things that bring it into existence and then to ask as many questions as there are aspects of an event – to bring an event into being hmm?'

Devote myself
to askIng
queStions
Chance
determIned
answers'll oPen
my mind to worLd around
at the same tIme
chaNging my music
sElf-alteration not self-expression

Figure 1 Mesostic from 'Composition in Retrospect' (Cage, 1983: 132).
Courtesy of Wesleyan University Press

experience, and this experience is not only received by the ears but by the eyes too. An ear alone is not a being' (Cage, 1968: 31). As a corollary, chance techniques could be used to explore the morphology of non-sounding materials such as texts, gestures, and graphics *whilst still – at least for Cage – being music*.[15] He often composed his lectures in the same way as his sounding works to exemplify his artistic programme. Likewise, having 'tried charts of words based on a gamut of vowels and then made poems – as possibilities for vocal works – by tossing' as early as 1951, he followed his friend and former student Jackson Mac Low in applying chance procedures more rigorously to texts (notably Thoreau and Joyce) from the 1970s, alongside his many mesostics (Cage, 1981b, 1983; Mac Low, 2001). These texts were 'music, which is, Arnold Schoenberg used to say, a question of repetition and variation, variation itself being a form of repetition in which some things are changed and others not (Cage, 1988: vi)'.

One of the variables that Cage explored was the conventional systems for musical notation. Always meticulous in his presentation of scores, and having both a practical experience in design and a wide circle of artist friends, these became visual artworks in their own right. This shift was not in itself surprising: he had tried painting at the time he began composing, was friends with and collaborated with many artists, and his work was, especially earlier in his career, more sympathetically received by visual artists and performed in galleries than by musicians and their institutions. Already in the early 1940s he had composed

---

[15] The idea that music need not be purely sonic is implicit in the contrast of Cage's anecdotes. In one, Cage attributed his devotion to music to Schoenberg: that his teacher accepted him as a pupil on condition that he dedicated his life to music; and that he vowed to do so when Schoenberg told his class that his goal in teaching was 'to make it impossible for [them] to write music'. These differ significantly with his early decision not to pursue architecture as he 'would have had to give his life to [that] alone', whereas he had many interests.

Figure 2 John Cage. Photographer: © Betty Freeman. Photo courtesy of the John Cage Trust

Chess Pieces for a gallery show of chess-related art, hand-drawn 'in black and white ink within the squares of a coloured chessboard, to be hung on the walls as a painting' (Silverman, 2010 [e-book]).

For his twenty-five year retrospective in 1958, New York's Stable Gallery presented an exhibition of the *Concert for Piano and Orchestra*, which incorporated eighty-four different notational techniques for the piano solo alone, reviewed by both *Art News* and *The New York Times*. For the same gallery, he initiated *Notations* (1968) in collaboration with Alison Knowles as an exhibition and art book showing the diversity of contemporary musical scores. The following year, after Duchamp's death, he created his first dedicated visual art project, *Not Wanting to Say Anything About Marcel* – two lithographs and silk screen printing on Plexiglass panels – again using chance procedures (Austin and Kahn, 2011: 230–3). Attracted by these, Kathan Brown invited Cage to work at her Crown Point Press in California, where he made works each year from 1978 to 1992; Ray Kass likewise brought him to the Mountain Lake Workshop in 1988 and 1990 to make watercolours, again applying musical transformations to material processes (Kass, 2001; Brown, 2002). Meanwhile his TV collaboration with Nam June Paik, *good morning mr. orwell*, broadcast simultaneously from New York, San Francisco, and Paris, with hook-ups in Germany and South Korea on New Year's Day 1984, reached an audience of more than ten million.

Cage's work sold well, exhibited at Leo Castelli (New York) and at Westkunst (Cologne); his first solo exhibition as an artist came in 1984 at Kettle's Yard (Cambridge). By the early 1990s, celebrated both for his own work and for his legendary associations with artists across much of the century, he was invited to curate a number of exhibitions (Belford, 2020). At the Mattress Factory, Pittsburgh, he installed forty-eight works by himself, Dove Bradshaw, and two other artists alongside seven chairs, using the *I Ching* each morning to determine which fifteen works to show, or walls to leave blank, the number of chairs to be available and where they should be placed – an exhibition morphology, like 'any living system', he said. The same process was adopted by curator Julie Lazar for *Rolywholover* (Los Angeles' MOCA, 1992), incorporating works and objects by Cage and artists associated with him, as well as unannounced performances throughout the gallery space. Invited as a guest curator at the Neue Pinakothek, Munich, by Ulrich Bischoff (Curator, Staatsgalerie Moderner Kunst), Cage conceived *museumcircle* by asking collaborating local museums with specialist collections to submit lists of objects they were willing to show, and using chance operations to create a constantly changing variety:

> Ordinarily when we go to an exhibition, we go to see one kind of thing. Whereas in this case, one saw a great variety of things in the museum space. It was very refreshing. The museum directors were very pleased, because they all knew their own collections *too* well. They were glad to see them brought into conjunction with things they didn't know at all.
>
> (Retallack, 1996: 141)

The same principle of establishing a counterpoint of independent elements or variables can be seen in his compositional processes of 'interpenetration' and 'indeterminacy', adopted in particular in his performances. Cage worked closely with dancers and choreographers from early in his career. Not only had they staged his percussion music – starting with Bonnie Bird (a pupil of Martha Graham's) in 1938 – but also the need for a more portable and flexible means for accompanying dance mothered his invention of the prepared piano. It was in teaching percussion music for dance that he met Merce Cunningham, first as a student and participant in his percussion ensemble, then later as collaborator and life partner. Cage acted as music director for Cunningham's dance company and was an inspiration in the choreographer's aesthetic and use of chance procedures.

Given his musical search for techniques to structure and to form sounds in time without relations of dependency, it was necessary to avoid simply accompanying dancers such that a composition would be experienced as determined by or merely supporting their movements. The solution was to accept the dance as a distinct yet simultaneous production, a counterpoint of *independent* systems. This would famously become the principle of his working methodology with Cunningham, but also opened the way towards 'theatre' whilst letting go of art's medium specificity. Rather than a *Gesamtkunstwerk* or amalgamation of several *different* art forms, the procedure of interpenetration implied a mutual affection by which each element – whilst separate – was changed through time by its proximity to the others.

Cage and Cunningham experimented further with this way of working whilst teaching at Black Mountain College in 1952. Inspired in part by Artaud's *The Theatre and Its Double*, which he took to confirm the idea that 'sound, gesture, music, lights, movement, words, [and] cries . . . could all "operate equally"', this featured both Cage (delivering a lecture) and dancers led by Cunningham alongside readings by the poet Charles Olson and writer MC Richards, music played by David Tudor, and all-white paintings by Rauschenberg. Whether it justified its legendary status as the first Happening or not, this principle was nevertheless influential in Cage's teaching, not least for Allan Kaprow and the artists who became associated with Fluxus.

Cage's exploration of the relations between the principle of interpenetration and his formal concern for morphology marked the shift in his later practice that broke decisively with the work-concept and its aesthetic. He elaborated this in 'Indeterminacy', the second of his Darmstadt lectures (1958), which indicated the direction his work was to take into the 1960s. Observing that a work might be composed using chance yet determined for performance (and, by implication, conventional for concert practice), he critiqued his own and others' works with social analogies. For example, his *Music of Changes* required its performer to operate like a building contractor following an architect's blueprint. This separation of mental from practical labour introduced an intolerable dualism into the musical situation, which could be overcome in part by making the acts of composition and performance – as also production and reception – not only overlap but also effectively *synchronous*. Musical time would then be inseparable from the temporality of its occasion.

By implication, composing the performance situation extended the range of variables that might be incorporated. For example, performers could be separated spatially to allow their sounds to 'be [their] own centre' and so to interpenetrate unconditioned by prior orders of relation. That is, interpenetration could operate as a variable principle within a situation opened to compositional morphology.

The performance would not be 'contained' – let alone overdetermined – by the context. By denying a correlation between events he aimed to avoid any implicit predication of a 'higher' or 'internal' principle – an intention, referential meaning, or aesthetic model – that would govern the relation.[16]

Lastly, as in his example of Christian Wolff's *Duo II for Pianists*, which was structured like a relay race with each performer cueing the other at indeterminate times, this required a compositional simplification towards a propositional form that could be enacted – not improvised – in the moment of its performance.[17] Without claiming a causal relation, it is perhaps not entirely accidental that George Brecht invented and refined the Event Score, a key development for Fluxus and precursor to Conceptual Art (and to curatorial concepts such as Hans Ulrich Obrist, Christian Boltanski and Bertrand Lavier's *Do It*), whilst studying with Cage at the New School for Social Research in 1958–9.[18]

He began to explore precisely these implications from the 1960s, firstly creating compositional tools or 'utilities' that could generate different works in diverse mediums – such as the template for the tape collage piece *Fontana Mix* (1958) being redeployed for *Theatre Piece* (1960) – then dramatised by *0'00"* (1962). Dedicated to his former student Toshi Ichiyanagi and his then artist wife, Yoko Ono (who had also visited his New School class), this comprised of the simple instruction, 'In a situation provided with maximum amplification (no feedback), perform a disciplined action'. The day after its premiere, he added four conditions (making five in all): that the action fulfil an obligation to others; that it be unique to that occasion, and not be a performance of music; and that the performer pay no attention to the situation. For example, Cage's 1965 performance at Brandeis University involved him writing correspondence, seated on a creaking chair whilst taking occasional sips of water, amplified by contact microphones.

---

[16] It was this principle, I suggest (contra Piekut, 2011: chapter 4; Lewis, 2015), rather than any latent misogyny or racism that precipitated confrontations between Cage and politically charged 'interpretations' of his music by Charlotte Moorman and Julius Eastman.

[17] Cage has been taken to task for his insistence on indeterminacy and disinterest in improvisation and jazz (Lewis, 2007; Feisst, 2009). In practice, I argue, this comes from a misunderstanding of the philosophical import of his practice and its anarchic political form.

[18] *Do It* (ironically echoing Nike's ad campaign) began as a conversation between the two artists and curator in 1993 – the year after Cage's death, and with a striking similarity to his late curatorial work – about 'how exhibition formats could be rendered more flexible and open-ended. This discussion led to the question of whether a show could take "scores," or written instructions by artists, as a point of departure, each of which could be interpreted anew every time they were enacted' (Obrist, 2020). On scoring's use for situational work and in visual art more broadly, see the contributions by Pablo Helguera and Carlos Basualdo in Jackson and Marincola (2020).

Far from being an aberration signalling 'a clear line of stylistic demarcation', a move away from the musical towards 'performance art', or simply a pragmatic solution to the increased demands on his time – as James Pritchett suggests – this shift in his practice was not a rupture but a *further transformation* of his concern for musicality.

> Implicit in [*4'33"*] . . . is that the movements can be of any length. I think that what we need in the field of music is a very long performance of that work. It is the fulfilment of my obligations in some way to other people, and I wanted to show that doing something that is not music is music.
>
> (Kostelanetz, 1988: 100)

At face value, *0'00"* mimics the type of instruction score Ono had developed in her collection *Grapefruit*, and presented in her New York loft – notably by La Monte Young, Henry Flynt, Nam June Paik, and Tony Conrad. It is certainly a simplified proposition. The conditions Cage added, however, extended his concern for controlling the interrelation of variables afforded by composing not only with sounds but also with the performance situation, such that previously 'extra-musical' aspects like the audience relation became compositional concerns. The 'fulfilment of an obligation to others', for example, linked his concern for formal discipline allowing sounds to 'be themselves' to his increasing attention to 'devotion' as the exemplification of disinterested acts that issue from their own centres – hence also the injunctions against repetition, of implicating a relation to musical tradition, or of staging or theatricalising a relation to audiences. Meanwhile the use of amplification introduced an element of indeterminacy into the moment of performance by making involuntary movements audible, or at least inhibiting the ability of a performer to control fully the sounds of their actions – simultaneously making intentional and necessary the unintended and contingent. Where *4'33"* demonstrated the impossibility of silence, *0'00"* showed there was no such thing as non-activity. The performed task was, furthermore, the undertaking of a promise to others, and therefore not only implicated in actions both prior and subsequent to the event, neither a beginning nor an end in itself, but also enmeshed in a *social* system of mutual obligations constitutive of community.[19]

This marked a shift from composing works to designing systems for making events that were at once formal interventions into social structures, exemplifications

---

[19] In contrast to the immunity of the sovereign individual, freed from the *munus* – the obligation, task, or duty – to others, the community (*com-munitas*) is formed by the network of relations and their dependencies. 'The person who is immune is the one who has been freed of the debt that not only is owed to the community but also forms the community's cohesion' (Hamilton, 2013: 39).

of actions as simultaneously independent *and* interpenetrating, and technologically mediated networks relating the part of individual actions to the social whole.[20] Cage's musicality was now less 'about' time – making change audible through a morphology of sounds – and increasingly an articulation of relations *through* time (Kostelanetz, 1988: 69).

The addressee of Cage's letter from his Brandeis performance is unknown, but the following month he wrote to the three writers – and friends – whose work now fired his imagination asking that they might each donate a lecture for his non-profit platform, Contemporary Performance Arts: systems theorist Buckminster Fuller; media theorist Marshall McLuhan; and New Left social philosopher Norman O. Brown (Cage, 2016: 319–25). It should be clear by now that this by no means signalled a move away from musical issues, but that it was *because of his musical concerns* for the temporal production of relations that he turned to thinkers addressing ideas of technologically mediated social systems. The corollary of musical time was a social practice that might articulate the musicality of collaboration, teamwork, and interdependence: 'How many people can work together happily, not just efficiently – happily and unselfishly? A serious question which the future of music will help to answer' (Cage, 1974/ 1979: 186).

In parallel with other musicians taking experimental approaches to composition, his work from this period onwards – including his lectures and publications – explored a wide range of musical possibilities for composing systems that might transform the situation of their presentation. Audiences became performers in projects like *33¹ᐟ³* (University of California, Davis, 1969), in which 300 LPs of various genres were provided with 12 stereo phonographs on tables around an otherwise empty hall for visitors to play as they chose (a precursor for Christian Marclay's art installation *The Sounds of Christmas*). For *Les Chants de Maldoror Pulvérisés par l'Assistance Même* (1971), extracts from Lautréamont's novel were distributed, with audience members voting on how the text should be read. The instructions permitted minority rule and specified approved methods for rebellion. Applying the principle to the manufactured record for the Nonesuch release of *HPSCHD* (1969), Cage's collaborator Lejaren Hiller generated *KNOBS*: 10,000 unique permutations – one for each record – for mixing the sound on home stereos.

---

[20] This marks a significant precedent for the development of 'systems esthetics', championed by Jack Burnham in his 1970 exhibition *Software*, and network compositions such as Cage's *Variations VII* – with ten telephones connected to locations around New York – and Robert Ashley's *String Quartet Describing the Motion of Large Real Bodies*, the score for which is a drawing of a circuit connection and instructions rendering its community of forty-three performers and string quartet as a social system.

Performers, too, became actors within the social drama of their own structures. For *Etcetera* (1973), orchestra members of the Opéra Français were invited to choose between being 'governed' by one of three conductors or moving to autonomous spaces where they could play independently. At other times, as with the cello concerto version of *108* (1991), the conductor was removed altogether leaving ensemble and soloist to negotiate the musical space without an external agent to impose order.

Whilst some of Cage's works wore their politics more overtly, like the *Lecture on the Weather* (1975), his primary concern was for musical events in which actions might be liberated from rules that both preceded and governed them – the same principles that had freed sounds of hierarchical and determinate relations. Just as the formal operation of controlling relations between variables allowed for a metamorphic temporalisation of sounds, enabling each to emanate from its own centre, extending this to the social situation invited actions to become both independent *and* interpenetrating, mutually affected. Such 'anarchic harmony' could then exemplify a revolutionary process of transformation in action. 'We need first of all a music in which not only are sounds just sounds but in which people are just people, not subject, that is, to laws established by any one of them, even if he is "the composer" or "the conductor"' (Cage, 1973: Foreword, 1988: vii).

Cage took the opportunity afforded him as Visiting Research Professor at the University of Illinois to stage a large-scale event embodying this principle, creating his first *Musicircus* (1967 – Figure 3) in the Stock Pavilion, normally used for showing cattle. A variety of musicians – including David Tudor, Gordon Mumma, an ensemble led by Salvatore Martirano, and two jazz bands – were invited to perform independently and simultaneously, whilst he operated the lighting console amplified by contact microphones, all joined by films and slides, balloon floats, and the sale of popcorn and cider. Whilst the piece had no instructions, variables of the situation were still carefully considered and managed: performances were given without hierarchy, without specifying genre or category, and were presented non-commercially and free of charge over a period of time without clear beginning or end. More than 5,000 people attended (Pritchett, 1993: 156–9; Brooks, 2002: 221).

This approach provided Cage with an exemplar for his musicalisation of the social. The jamboree around the performance of *HPSCHD* (Figure 4) featured fifty-nine amplifiers and loudspeakers – the largest number ever used to that date, he believed – eleven 100' × 40' screens for eight motion pictures, and sixty-four slide projectors, amongst other attractions, experienced by around 7,000 visitors. 'Municipal compositions' – means to make a city 'audible to itself' – began with *49 Waltzes for Five Boroughs* (1977); whilst *HMCIEX*, created

Figure 3 John Cage, *MUSICIRCUS* (University of Illinois, Champaign-Urbana, Stock Pavilion, 17 November 1967). Photo courtesy of the John Cage Trust

for the 1984 Los Angeles Olympics, comprised a Musicircus of folk music from the 151 participating countries. Even ways of living could be musicalised: approached in 1990 by a group of squatters in Hanau, East Berlin, Cage used a map of the area to create a chance-derived list of places, dates, and times to record sounds. The brochure accompanying their resulting record, *Five Hanau Silence*, drew the parallel – just as 'all sounds are equal', so this community intended 'to live a life without domination'.

In these and other examples, Cage's late practice opened a way towards what I am calling 'curatorial composing' that was no longer governed or regulated by the work-concept. It was neither concerned with music's essence or 'medium specificity' nor with its autonomy from social life. His working method of affording the interpenetrating and indeterminate relations between independent variables can be understood as a continuation and further extension of Schoenberg's system of developing variation, a *musical* procedure operating beyond conventional musical materials. Form and content were elaborated as 'the continuity of a morphology', as Cage put it, without a foundational, a priori, or elementary condition.

It is important to note, however, that Cage was not the only composer innovating in the musical production of public situations. The Greek composer Jani Christou, for example, developed his complementary methods of 'continuum'

Figure 4 John Cage, *HPSCHD* (University of Illinois, Champaign-Urbana, Assembly Hall, 6 May 1969). Photo courtesy of the John Cage Trust

and 'metapraxis' also in the 1960s as techniques concerned with transformation – or 'musical energetics' – in particular the irruption into habitual, cyclical, or conventional temporal experience of something unprecedented, irregular, and unpredictable. In parallel with Cage, his concern for non-foundational logic and compositional variation can be appreciated from his studies in philosophy with Wittgenstein and Bertrand Russell and his Schoenbergian private composition lessons from the Alban Berg specialist Hans Ferdinand Redlich. By the late 1960s, Christou was no longer composing works but developing frameworks for ritualised events inviting and acknowledging public participation, such as *Epicycle* (1968). For its premiere at the Hellenic Week of Contemporary Music, Christou constructed an event – scored through drawings and instructions – that lasted a day but could have any duration, 'days, weeks, months, years'. The activities initiated through these principles could likewise 'take place not only in conventional areas of performance, but anywhere, depending on the work: outside the auditorium, in public squares, in the streets of a city, anywhere' (Christou, 1968: 150). The score itself indicates the possibility of organising it in 'other manifestations, such as exhibitions, seminars, conferences and so on', with licence for 'soundless performance' if such conditions resulted in objections to its audibility. More recently, the possibilities implied by Christou's practice were explored by the curatorial team for documenta14 (Szymczyk, 2017), who also followed closely the potential to incorporate organisational principles from Pauline Oliveros' *Sonic Meditations* (1974) and other text scores (McKeon, 2021).

In short, curatorial composing was not 'founded' by Cage. It does not 'originate' with him, or with him alone, but arose from immanent concerns with musical logic. His is also not the only musical method, as I will show in elaborating Heiner Goebbels' practice. Indeed, Cage's project retained a level of abstraction based on the dialectical principle of negation, leaving several issues at best only obliquely addressed. For example, applied to the public domain, the anarchic notion of people as sovereign and independent individuals whose actions interpenetrate to construct the social fabric obscured concrete realities of the ways crowds form and operate, and of how identities are not sovereign but often politically imposed. As a concern for unmediated temporal experience, his musical logic avoided or effaced the roles of memory and affects in the production of meaning. Language was problematic for Cage, a medium best enjoyed when musicalised. When confronting 'found' cultural objects – whether texts or, as with *Apartment House 1776* (1976), early American music – he preferred to decouple them from any hierarchical affiliation to their referents or original usage. That is, his method was vulnerable to the encroachment of unanticipated meanings and variables that might short-circuit the encounter with complexity that he aimed for, and disavowed the subjective play of *desire* for reference, meaning, and closure. It is to these issues – of the role of cultural 'readymades', of a plurality of individuals and the phenomenology of 'crowds', and of the affective production of meaning – that I now turn to in addressing Goebbels' approach to curatorial composing.

4 Heiner Goebbels: Questioning Authority

> All arts bring to their renewal urgent impulses from outside, from elements not only addressing current trends but questioning their own laws.
>
> *(Goebbels, 1997/2002: 138 – my translation)*

Heiner Goebbels belongs nowhere, and that suits him fine. Attempts to categorise his practice, to pigeon-hole it, invariably fail. He is difficult to pin down. He writes scored works and is represented by a music publisher; nevertheless, the opinion that he's 'really a theatre director' is quite common in music circles, at least in the United Kingdom. He is often cited as a pioneer of 'postdramatic theatre' – a term introduced by his then colleague Hans-Thies Lehmann (2006) – yet this is a paradigm that explicitly deconstructs the conventions of repertoire theatre, in particular the privileged roles of play texts in staging parallel realities and of actors in representing characters. More precisely, his practice is exemplary for studies of the *musicalisation* of theatre (Rebstock and Roesner, 2012; Roesner, 2014). On a number of occasions he has been invited to make installations for galleries, though his work is not – at least not yet – recognised by the art market and collectors. From 2012 to 2014 he was appointed the Artistic Director and Managing Director of the Ruhrtriennale, one of Europe's largest arts festivals, though this is the one and only time he has taken up such an invitation and so also provides my focus.[21]

In what follows, my aim is therefore not simply to create a more expansive category that might contain his practice, or to bracket him under the label of 'curatorial composing'. This is emphatically not an exercise in creating a new 'Cage School' and placing Goebbels within it, nor one of initiating a 'Goebbels School' even whilst recognising his influence on theorists of performance curation.[22] Rather, I want to acknowledge the specificity of his practice – what provides consistency across seemingly diverse fields of work – whilst drawing from it themes and issues that bear directly on the matter of musicality beyond the work-concept.

A further challenge is to avoid constructing a narrative of Goebbels as the 'author' of a body of work that somehow exemplifies my subject, not least because the work-concept itself was – as Goehr notes – instituted on the principle of composers' authorship of original works. This can be implicit when introducing an artist biographically, as if writing a character on the page with an impression of psychological depth, of intention expressed in finished objects such as texts or scores, and charting a narrative of progress to 'maturity' and 'mastery'. As I will show, Goebbels deliberately confounds structures of authorship to raise instead the question of *authority*; that is, he is fundamentally concerned with how meaningful encounters can be composed without recourse

---

[21] Between 1982 and 1985, he also created, produced, and organized (with Christoph Anders) a 'MATERIALAUSGABE – Veranstaltungsreihe mit musikalischem Risiko' – ('Performance Series with Musical Risk') – at Batschkapp, a venue in Frankfurt. These monthly performances included the first Frankfurt shows of Einstürzende Neubauten, Minus Delta T, Tödliche Doris, John Zorn, Arto Lindsay, Christian Marclay, Fred Frith, David Moss, David Garland, Nick Cave, Glenn Branca, and many others. The series ended with a 'Materialausgabe Compilation' one-hour special event at the Moers Festival, with sixty artists on three stages, each performing one minute. (Email to the author, 28 March 2022)

[22] Florian Malzacher, one of the pioneers of performance curation in theory and in practice, studied at the Institute of Applied Theatre Studies in Giessen, where Goebbels was a distinguished Professor and a leading practitioner between 1999 and 2018, and Managing Director from 2002 until 2011 (Goebbels, 2018a).

to a first principle, transcendental concept, original intention, or foundational building block. In this chapter, then, I will present a brief chronology of the paths his practice has taken to draw out key aspects that inform his role with the Ruhrtriennale and that are significant for curatorial composing.[23]

Goebbels turned sixteen in 1968, the year that promised to contest all authorities. He studied sociology in Frankfurt in the early 1970s at the famous department established by Max Horkheimer and Theodor Adorno, becoming a young combatant of the 'Sponti' movement with fellow activists such as Daniel Cohn-Bendit – one of the student leaders of the May '68 protests in France and later influential MEP – and living in the same block (a squat of four joint buildings) as Joschka Fischer, who went on to become a leader within the Green Party before serving as Germany's Foreign Minister under Gerhard Schröder's SDP-Green coalition (1998–2005).

It was after reading Eisler's 'Conversations About Brecht' (1975/2014) that Goebbels was inspired to turn to music. Following his diploma in sociology with studying music at the conservatory, he went on to arrange Eisler's songs for the political street band he co-founded – the Sogenanntes linksradikales Blasorchester (the 'so-called left-radical wind band'), named after a public jibe – then riffing on them in his improvising duo with saxophonist Alfred Harth. Joined by vocalist Christoph Anders and drummer Chris Cutler to form the band Cassiber, samples of Eisler's teacher Arnold Schoenberg amongst others were incorporated into a mutant rock ('I wouldn't consider us a rock group; we were too weird' – Goebbels and Gourgouris, 2004: 12).[24] Composition was both collective and improvised, not authored. Furthermore, nothing arrived ex nihilo: material came from individual and collective memory, shaped in song form, often drawing on texts by Chris Cutler or others (such as Thomas Pynchon's writing used in their album *A Face We All Know*).

Collaborative creation and production were also a feature of Goebbels' experience with dance and theatre companies, notably his long association with Heiner Müller (before he became Brecht's successor as a director of the Berliner Ensemble). Establishing the sampler as an instrument in its own right, he extensively explored the possibilities for appropriating and using found sounds as an intertextual medium and as a means for musicalising text. Writing in 1988, he claimed that the avant-garde totem of originality was now a dead letter: not only had the 'progressive' mining of raw musical materials effectively exhausted its seams, but also the modernist social model and

---

[23] For a concise overview of Goebbels' work, see also Ramović (2018).

[24] This formation of a band can also be related to Eisler's 'serious challenge' to composers, 'to try to write in popular genres that don't have [a conventional] hackneyed banality' (Eisler, 1975/2014: 14).

philosophy – the work-concept – which had sustained that approach had passed. Musical innovation had consequently shifted from the concert hall to the disco scene, experimental rock, and improvised music, especially in New York. The world had moved on: 'the time for personal styles is over' (Goebbels, 1988/ 2002: 206 – my translation).[25]

The composer was therefore not the author of a message to be correctly translated, interpreted, or understood. For Goebbels, the task was to explore the *musical* production of meaning from these pre-existing or codified layers and fragments. It was by developing a syntax with samples, a means of composing with sounds *as a language* – not simply as another mode of narration or system of reference, but suspending signification whilst allowing the potential for meaning – that he then developed the hybrid form of the *Hörstück*, a theatre of the ears, through counterpoint and film-like techniques of collage, montage, close-up, cut, and dissolve.[26]

Goebbels went further in transposing this method into a new model of 'scenic concert'. These staged events often incorporated musicians playing from their own traditions and techniques, variously including an improvising group featuring Don Cherry, George Lewis, Fred Frith, Arto Lindsay, Tim Berne, and Charles Hayward, among others (*The Man in the Elevator*, 1987); the speed metal crossover band Megalomaniax (*Wolokolamsker Chausée*, 1989); Senegalese griots Boubakar and Sira Djebate (*Ou bien le débarquement désastreux*, 1993); the Mondriaan Quartett playing Shostakovich, Ravel, Bach, Bryars, and others (*Eraritjaritjaka*, 2004); the Hilliard Ensemble vocal quartet (*I Went to the House but Did Not Enter*, 2008); and the Vocal Theatre Carmina Slovenica (*When the Mountain Changed Its Clothing*, 2012).

> Essentially, my pieces are different because I work with various ensembles, bands, musicians, and singers and give them their own space. I consider it old-fashioned to believe one has to create everything oneself – that's a nineteenth-century concept – or that one has something inside that has to come out. It doesn't work that way with me. There's nothing inside me that's crying to come out. I have the impression that I work more like an architect. I want to know what materials are available to me, why a particular house has to be built, who is going to want to live in it, what their needs are, and whether I can build rooms for them. I must know what's standing next to the house, in front of it and behind it. I must also know the person giving me the

---

[25] See also Eisler's 1935 essay 'Some Remarks on the Situation of the Modern Composer' (Eisler, 1999, 106–113), and his statement that 'in bourgeois aesthetics they talk about an "artistic personality." In the workers' music movement we do not aspire to "style" but to new methods of musical technique' (Eisler 1999: 59).

[26] Goebbels distinguishes this from the *Hörspiel*, regarding this latter as a staged play recorded for microphones.

commission. Only if all of these conditions are relatively restricted, can I start to respond to them. (Goebbels, 1995)

It was a step – not a leap – from here to compose the programme of the Ruhrtriennale and to direct (as *Regisseur*) whole 'works' of others, one each year alongside a further major work annually with invited directors. These were specifically bold and large-scale music theatre projects 'which have a radical potential to basically question the conventional assumptions of the genre itself', and so were absent from the repertoire of opera houses.[27] Many of these productions were therefore the work's first staging since premiering decades before, and included Cage's *Europeras 1 and 2* alongside Lemi Ponifasio's direction of Carl Orff's *Prometheus* in 2012; Harry Partch's *Delusion of the Fury* with Romeo Castellucci's presentation of Morton Feldman's *Neither* in 2013; and Louis Andriessen's *De Materie* alongside Robert Wilson's staging of Helmut Lachenmann's *Mädchen mit den Schwefelhölzern* in 2014.

Before focusing on his direction of *De Materie* in particular, I want to highlight two aspects of Goebbels' practice that address the matter of authority (or value) which, as I noted, is foundational to the work-concept. Firstly, Goehr emphasises that the work-concept is integral to 'medium specificity', to works *of music*. Goebbels' practice corrodes this. He is not a 'Jack of all trades' but adopts a consistent method – a compositional technique – across supposedly discrete artistic disciplines. There are parallels with Cage's principle of inter-penetration, of independent systems such as choreography, lighting, and music interweaving together, but Goebbels takes a further step. Each discipline – dance, music, visual art, or theatre – is *already* hybrid, already involves or implies the others but does so by privileging one quality, whether gesture and movement, sound, image, or text. Discrete forms of art can in this way be understood as conventions for producing meaning through hierarchical ordering of materials. The technique of interpenetration separates different mediums to avoid the subordination of any one element to another but it does not address directly the ways that these hierarchical systems continue to structure the *desire* for meaning, to reimpose order on the perceptual field. Goebbels acknowledges and holds these medium-specific systems in tension polyphonically such that at each moment one aspect may appear to 'lead' the others, like voices in counterpoint.

Goebbels develops the social implications of this in his essay 'Against the Gesamtkunstwerk: On the differences of the arts' (1997/2002 – my transla-tion). 'The classical stage arts are based on a hierarchy', he observes, with

---

[27] Email to the author, 28 March 2022.

a central category that expands to incorporate others on its 'periphery'. This structure of dominance in which the arts, whilst individual, 'usually submit to each other . . . doesn't stop in front of the spectators [but] leaps off the stage to overwhelm and patronise the audience', inhibiting their capacity to experience on their own terms. As a mode of production, the director is sovereign, dominating the scene and treating 'his assistants like inferior servants'. Everything is directed towards his intended meaning, such that text, gesture, costumes, scenery, lighting, music, and sound are harnessed to an idea external to their own power, doubling each other such that 'what we see here is repeated at least seven times'.

In direct contrast to such a *Gesamtkunstwerk*, 'the sacrifice of each individual art for the purpose of the whole', Goebbels' states his aim 'for each art to be mutually detached in a continuous state of suspension', creating an open situation – likewise for the audience as a gathering of individuals – in which 'theatre' becomes 'a place of experience (and entertainment, of course), not a classroom'. Avoiding any 'Wagnerian claim for wholeness', he seeks 'a questioning feeling, a productive incompleteness, a new model for communication. *The mediation process itself must become a theme of art*'. [Der Vermittlungsprozeß selbst muß zum Thema der Kunst werden.]

Two points need to be emphasised here. On the one hand, where the work-concept constitutes music's essence as an *internal* core, Goebbels deconstructs this to demonstrate that it is a social convention or norm, and so already *external*. Music is in this sense a construct and so inseparable from the public that hears it as such. The principle of autonomy no longer holds. On the other hand, the 'mediation process itself' is a key concern of the curatorial. The role of museum and gallery curators is fundamentally involved with articulating encounters between publics and significant objects through which meaning is established. The shift that Goebbels makes is to acknowledge and prepare for the creative role of audiences. That audiences play an active role in shaping events – in creating 'atmosphere', in the forming of affect and the production of meaning – is a common experience for musicians, especially improvisers. As a corollary, value and authority do not precede the public encounter – as an inherent quality of works – but become a product of it. I develop this further below with the aid of Arendt.

For now, it is important to note that Goebbels *composes* this process, weaving together different elements and equally differentiated audience members and their expectations. Indeed, it is exactly in this sense that he invokes Hanns Eisler's aphorism that 'whoever only understands music, doesn't understand even that'. Not only does this follow Eisler's lesson that music is never 'pure' but always already political; it is also 'apt in a very general artistic sense'. 'You can't see music only as a component – albeit a component of equal value – of theatre. There's much more to music than that' (Eisler, 1975/2014: 69).

Secondly, whilst the work-concept instituted composers as 'authors' of works, Goebbels is adamant that this is no longer adequate. His practice is collaborative and the encounters he stages result from lengthy processes of improvisation. Moreover, 'the composer is no longer the discoverer, the master of his sounds, but rather the *subject* of sounds that precede him' (Goebbels, 1996/2002: 181 – my translation). Following the deconstructive lesson that words refer to other words before they denote any worldly object (as observed with dictionary definitions), 'musical' sounds similarly refer to idioms, genres, techniques, and repertoires of musical practice and signification. Not only does this allow for composition to include the work of other musicians and artists – as a curator might incorporate the work of several artists in a group show – but also the composer as author is once more, as with music's 'medium specificity', a social construct.

These two aspects of curatorial composing were evident in Goebbels' approach to his role as the Ruhrtriennale's Artistic Director. For example, in his opening year Michal Rovner's *Current* and the exhibition *12 Rooms* (curated by Hans Ulrich Obrist and Klaus Biesenbach) provided exemplars for Goebbels' assertion that the 'distinctions between the performing arts and contemporary visual art have become increasingly difficult to maintain' (Goebbels, 2012).[28] The following year, he emphasised precisely those experiences 'when language takes a step back' and that instead 'confront us with those forces which evade recognition, accessibility and manipulation; forces which are beyond our reach and above all resist personification' (Goebbels, 2013).

In programming, he not only presented artists, ensembles, and groups with ready-made works but also brought in some of his own collaborators to lead on production and to work closely with invited artists and companies. This was not to position himself as a 'meta-artist' appropriating the work of others, nor simply as a 'programmer', but composing a festival form that made the question of authorship *subordinate* to the public encounters it enabled.[29] Unlike his predecessors – founding director Gerard Mortier (2002–4), Jürgen Flimm (2005–8), and Willy Decker (2009–11) – Goebbels adopted no theme, message,

---

[28] The project was a co-commission between Manchester International Festival – where it opened in 2011 as *11 Rooms* – and the Ruhrtriennale under Goebbels' direction. Not only did it expand on its first edition, for example with the inclusion of an installation by the choreographer Xavier Le Roy, it also featured a different work by Lucy Raven, *Room Tone* (2012), appropriating and distorting composer Alvin Lucier's classic work, *I Am Sitting In A Room*.
[29] Interview with Goebbels, 12 October 2018.

medium, or overarching idea for the programme.[30] Nor were the artists and works presented purely in line with his 'taste', at least not as an outward expression of an inner sentiment. Alongside a substantial diversification of the programme across the arts (notably with dance and installed artwork), his introductions to the festival brochures emphasised rather a disposition to experiences that lacked definition or the guarantees provided by a conceptual frame – to the new, the unknown and unfamiliar, the hybrid and uncategorisable, to collaborative work, and to artistic experiences that manifest their own 'independent reality', non-representational, without 'make-believe' or prior guarantee of understanding.

> For a strong artistic experience we need an encounter with something that we *don't* know: an unseen image, an unheard sound, a seemingly impossible movement ... All this, I think, can be offered by the Ruhrtriennale as an international festival of the arts – and I'm certain that our public is curious.
> (Goebbels, 2012: 7–11 – my translation)[31]

This approach is in stark contrast with most curatorial practices in the contemporary gallery arts, in which authorship is usually sovereign and in which all work may be bracketed by the 'postconceptual', as the material expression of an artist's concept. The curator is figured either as a kind of silent partner to the artists on display – especially for solo or duo shows – or, more often for group shows, becomes herself an author of the exhibition, signing it off like a work in its own right (McKeon, 2022b). The tension between curator and artists, and the proximity of creative – or 'performative' – curating to the approaches of artists' curating, has become a problematic characteristic of the field (Green, 2018). Even collective approaches to organising exhibitions and biennials are usually premised on conventions of authorship, such as a statement or theme, whilst provenance and the identity of artists involved plays a central role in the meanings and value they produce (Karp, 1990: 12).

The apparent paradox of Goebbels' curatorial position is that whilst authorship as such – as style, personal expression, taste, intentional statement, or

---

[30] Compare with www.ruhrtriennale.de/en/pQ6bUL/ruhrtriennale/archiv, accessed 19 October 2020.

[31] Dance, as the 'least institutionalized' form, featured strongly with Anne Teresa De Keersmaeker, Boris Charmatz, Mathilde Monnier, Jérôme Bel, La Ribot, William Forsythe, Saburo Teshigawara, and others, many with several productions over the three years. Musical theatre, film and music collaborations, and unconventional 'opera' provided a backbone, including – as a quick, indicative sample – Romeo Castellucci, Robert Wilson, Tim Etchells, Tarek Atoui, Rimini Protokoll, Robert LePage, Massive Attack with Adam Curtis, Nature Theater of Oklahoma, and the Brothers Quay with the Arditti Quartet. Alongside *12 Rooms*, the group show of performance works, gallery-recognised artists were prominent with installations and performance collaborations, such as Michal Rovner, Ryoji Ikeda, Douglas Gordon, Mischa Kuball, Dan Perjovschi, Tino Sehgal, Antje Ehmann with Harun Farocki, and Christian Marclay.

efficient cause, whether of the artist or the curator – is deferred to incorporate the audience, the question of *authority* remains critical. In rejecting the two key conventions by which artistic authority is conventionally claimed and exercised – medium specificity (musical tradition) and the author function – as *external* constructs, he seeks an alternative model that is immanent to the encounter, which I elaborate in Sections 5.3 and 5.4 through Arendt's philosophy. It is precisely the question of how authority might be understood once its status as 'unshaken cornerstone' collapses, its loss akin to losing 'the groundwork of the world', that she addresses (1961: 91–142).

Goebbels' acknowledgement that value is produced only in the public encounter echoes the democratising impulse of the New Museology in sharing the interpretive and meaning-making process with viewers (Robinson, 2020), yet – as I will show – does so through a distinct approach to the temporalities of production and encounter. Indeed, having declined previous offers to act as guest artistic director for other festivals, he accepted the opportunity at the Ruhrtriennale 'as an invitation for a *signature*, an invitation with all its freedom for a *different aesthetic*'.[32] Not only did the situation here afford a unique degree of freedom and ambition, it also required a 'very subjective' approach for 'the choice of productions, curation of artists, use of spaces, marketing, design', and so on.

> I took care of everything, watched and controlled also all print, word by word, even details in the design of the light at the venues. . . .I wanted to be generous to the artists and to the audience – on an eye-level – and I had the feeling this is quite a new territory.

This approach can best be understood as a means of taking responsibility for a latent 'authorship' with *deferred* authority– an 'empty signature', akin to an 'empty' or 'floating signifier' without a fixed referent. He 'signed' the Ruhrtriennale neither as a figure with whom the public might identify – just as he has emphatically argued against actors and performers portraying characters for audiences to empathise or relate to – nor as a 'headliner', but as a placeholder or guarantor for the potential in the encounters being staged, for the contact points between artistic preparation and audience experience.

Unlike the proper name that is separable from a person's being (a web search, for example, finds more than one Ed McKeon), Foucault (1998) showed that the 'author function' is bound to a singular body of work, securing it from a textual field that is not limited. It acts, he argued, as a regulatory principle or mechanism for containing meaning, notably at times of its unruly proliferation – as

---

[32] Email to the author, 11 November 2018. Emphasis in the original.

when meaning becomes 'merely subjective' and interpretations abound – by attaching qualified works to a circumscribed interiority. It binds a *corpus* of works to an origin or source in the intentional persona of their maker. Arendt noted how this *inherent* construct of authority emerged in classical Rome as the institution of Aristotle's principle that elders hold a 'natural' superiority over those yet to achieve maturity. This introduced into the political domain a problematic distinction specific to the 'pre-political' private sphere in which the family head claimed power (through a monopoly of violence if necessary). In this establishment of public seniority, authority (*auctoritas*) derived from *augere*, to augment, 'and what authority or those in authority always augment is the foundation. Those endowed with authority were the elders, the Senate or the *patres*, who had obtained it by descent and by transmission (tradition) from those who had laid the foundations . . . the ancestors' (Arendt, 1961: 122). This primal authority is therefore not inherent but always *external* and derivative to the public sphere in which it is exercised.

Goebbels' curatorial signature pointed neither to a foundational authority in the external past nor to assertions for his own creative property, but to an immanent *potential* authority to come. The programme retained the quality of a signature, sharing characteristics of those precepts Foucault identified with authored works: the programmed events can reasonably be considered of *constant* value, rationally *coherent*, stylistically *consistent*, and *contemporary* to their historicity – even whilst marked by their heterogeneity and, for the most part, abstraction from direct commentary on the present. In contrast to the author function, however, its authority was potential – directed to 'unknown' encounters – consequential, temporally deferred, and immanent to each experience. Foucault anticipated something of this, recognising that – as an *historical* fiction – the author function may change.

> 'I think that, as our society changes, at the very moment when it is in the process of changing, the author function will disappear, and in such a manner that fiction and its polysemous texts will once again function according to another mode . . . one that will no longer be the author but will have to be determined or, perhaps, experienced' (Foucault, 1998: 222).

Goehr's claims for the work-concept, that 'it is . . . a contingent, retroactively discovered, bonding and roping process' (Goehr, 2007: 108) – introduced earlier – apply to the incorporation of new creations as authored products. The crucial difference in the events Goebbels stages, as I will show, is that authority is *not* retrospective, understood as external and derivative, but an emergent quality of the encounter. It involves the immanent advent of what Arendt called the *space of appearance*. To appreciate this in action and so to provide an instance for further reflection, I turn now to Goebbels' production of *De Materie*, which I approach through a series of variations.

5 Spaces of Appearance

What characterizes the Ruhrtriennale are the interactions between artists and spaces. These make strong artistic experiences possible for all of us and they are my highest priority. *(Goebbels, 2014: 5–10)*

There are moments that stay: memories of extravagant strangeness; riddle-me realities hiding in plain view; encounters with a sensuous world returning our gaze, lending us an ear, disturbing time's flow.

In a cavernous former palace of German manufacturing, 160 m depth by 35 m width by 20 m height of light and shade, the Ensemble Modern Orchestra, seated, is silently and mechanically manoeuvred on its shifting platform from the mid-space to stage front. Playing continuously, their music phases from a Stravinsky inflected big-band boogie woogie – for a section inspired by Piet Mondrian – to chiming chords in a hovering pattern, reverberating and expectant, punctuating a time without destination. The space is resonant.

An enchanted stillness settles.

In the far distance, an illuminated motorised zeppelin, moon-faced towards the audience, rotates, stretching its light elliptically by its lateral trajectory (echoing the performance's opening gesture). A blue-white pool of light fades in and a hushed murmur ripples across the audience, revealing what our doubting ears could only a short while earlier disbelieve, but which our noses cannot mistake: a flock of 100 apparently untended sheep in 'centre stage'.

They bathe together in the light, unconcerned (Figure 5).

Remarkably quiet, leaving the music uncontested bar the rare bleat, this ungoverned community drifts peacefully together in greater or lesser clusters, staying within their illumined domain, holding the shape of a collective body. After a while, the orchestral chords begin to insist, the zeppelin moves slowly above and around them, and they shift further downstage together, chorusing, without stragglers.

The light dims, turns lunar red, and the sheep re-fold themselves.

Twilit, the music takes on an eerie, cinematic and portentous quality as the zeppelin circles. Eight members of ChorWerk Ruhr lament a sonnet on desire, death, and immortal love by the nineteenth-century Dutch poet Willem Kloos. The light returns to its midnight blue, and as the orchestra's harmonies sound a climactic alarm, the choir gives voice to its paean of undying heartache.

Figure 5 *De Materie*, Wonge Bergmann/Ruhrtriennale, courtesy of Heiner Goebbels

As if on cue, miraculously, the sheep begin to follow the zeppelin as it glides serenely into the far-distant and unseeable back stage, into darkness and legend.

Meanwhile, a set of the 1911 Solvay Conference (on radiation and the quanta) is rapidly assembled forestage for the final monologue, combining moments of Marie Curie's Nobel Prize-winning speech and diary entries in the wake of her husband's death. So concludes Goebbels' production of Andriessen's *De Materie*, an 'opera' – or rather, a symphonic essay, or tableau of ideas – manifestly exploring the relationships between matter and spirit, substance and subject, nature and culture, the one and the many, and between text, music, light, movement, and scenography.

For twenty minutes – or what feels like a moment unbounded – this ovine troupe has held the stage.

Presented over six evenings at the Kraftzentrale, Landschaftspark Duisburg-Nord in August 2014, this production – the first since the work's 1989 premiere staging by Robert Wilson – was a feature of Goebbels' third and final year as Artistic Director of the Ruhrtriennale. Eighteen months later, before re-producing *De Materie* with different musicians and a new flock at New York's Park Avenue Armory (2016) – and then without sheep as a 'staged concert' at the Opera of La Plata and at Teatro Colón, Buenos Aires (2017) – Goebbels included video documentation of this unshepherded segment on a loop in a space behind his larger video installation, *The Human Province*, at the Kunsthalle im Lipsiusbau, Dresden, a temporary exhibition space of the Staatliche Kunstsammlung.[33]

It is immediately apparent from this that issues of authorship and of the work have become moot. *De Materie* has become a catalyst for a variety of staged encounters, understood variously as music, theatre, performance spectacle, or gallery installation without privileging any form.

In the programme book, Goebbels remarks that he did not know the piece beforehand, though had followed Andriessen's work since the 1970s as a composer with whom he felt close. Orkest De Volharding – a brassy and jazzy line-up co-founded by the Dutch composer in 1972, initially as a street band with a political dimension – had provided a model and stimulus for the Sogenanntes linksradikales Blasorchester. Marking his seventy-fifth birthday in 2014, the production could thus straightforwardly be understood as a tribute.

Yet whilst *De Materie* is unquestionably by Andriessen, it is itself assembled from a variety of found texts – including several not conventionally 'authored', such as Marie Curie's diary entries – and the music makes no attempt to hide the historical models that enter the mix. Indeed, Andriessen underlines 'his conviction that music is always related to other music', using models contemporaneous with his found texts that themselves reference earlier forms. Part 4 for example, for which Goebbels presents our lunar idyll, draws on the anachronistic composition of a pavane – a slow, processional dance from the sixteenth century – from 1927 by his father, Hendrik Andriessen, echoing Kloos' untimely adoption of the sonnet (Coenan, 2014). That *De Materie* lacks 'a sense of organic unity', as John Rockwell (1989) lamented in his *New York Times* review of Wilson's original production, could be (and has been) attributed equally to much of Goebbels' work.

It is important to note that whilst dismantling the hierarchies of medium specificity and authorial conventions, for both *De Materie* and the Ruhrtriennale programme more broadly, Goebbels did not replace them with alternative 'interiorities' but engaged the various ways in which artists' work was already in dialogue with supposedly 'external' aspects of production. In a first set of reflections, then, I consider his approach to the sites and spaces in which the festival was held to elaborate the aesthetics of what Goebbels describes as an 'absent centre'.

---

[33] Running from 15 January to 10 April 2016, the main installation incorporated video documentation from fifty-four productions of his musical theatre work *Eraritjaritjaka*, featuring the actor Andre Wilms and based on texts by Elias Canetti (from whose work he adopted the exhibition's title). www.youtube.com/watch?v=cGYdoSq-7bk&feature=youtu.be, accessed 7 October 2020.

5.1 Sites of *Zeit*

The programme books for each year's festival under Goebbels' direction are desirable objects, A4 size with full-colour full-page images, as well as smaller installation, production, and artist photographs or reproductions on gloss paper. Like the publications produced for many biennales, they are designed to be kept. It is striking, then, that a feature of each brochure is the space given to the venues in which events were held. Unlike standard festival programmes, in which such information is entirely functional – usually limited to an address, a website link, and perhaps a map – larger spaces here are granted a double-page spread (Figure 6), including a featured image and a short history. These venues are 'stars of the show', just as much as the artists.

Launched in 2002, the Ruhrtriennale was conceived at a time of 'biennialisation', alongside the turn to heritage (Hartog, 2015), as an initiative aiming to stimulate cultural development with the decline of heavy industries and manufacturing, and to raise the North Rhine-Westphalia's international profile. The rehabilitation and repurposing of the region's industrial heritage was central to this, anticipated and prepared by the International Architectural Exhibition along the 18 km of the Emscher River in the Ruhr basin during the 1990s (World Architecture Community, 2016). Not only were these recovered landscapes intended to mark a changed relation to nature, influenced by the ecological movement and emergent green politics, they also adapted and learned from the shifting aesthetic appreciation of such alternative sites, emblematic and influentially displayed in the celebrated photographs of Ernst and Hilla Becher, professors at Düsseldorf Art School.

For Goebbels, this was familiar territory. Not only was he intimately aware of this art history – he has attended Documenta since its fourth edition, in 1968, aged sixteen; these buildings had provided a base for his own work.

> I hadn't been to the Ruhrtriennale, but I knew the buildings. I had a performance of *Black on White* in the Jahrhunderthalle [at Bochum] before the Ruhrtriennale existed.[34]

In contrast with the use of such spaces 'as a backdrop for . . . storytelling', he insists on an expanded site-specific approach (Kwon, 2002). The space itself acts on the event and does so – crucially – through at least three intertwining relations to time: the histories and logic of the site, its 'memory'; the form of production it affords as a precondition for the moment of the encounter; and the opening of an event to unpredictability and to an emerging world through its

---

[34] Interview with the author, 12 October 2018.

Figure 6 Ruhrtriennale brochure (Goebbels, 2014: 78–9). Photograph by Ed McKeon

publics. It is with these that Goebbels composes ('like an architect'), seeking a precise balance – without hierarchy, without *arkhē* or *telos* – between past and future, as Arendt put it. In contrast to the narration or representation of time, of a contemporary 'picture' or anachronism, he proposes an 'anachronic experience' offering 'a conversation across time' (Goebbels, 2019).

> I am interested in what evokes contrapuntal tensions *between* up and down, *between* right and left, *between* before and after, *between* what can be seen and what can be heard; *between* what you expect and what actually happens; *between* what you experience and what you may think about it; *between* what can be understood and what constructively defies understanding.
>
> (Goebbels, 2015: xxiii; emphasis added)

Site here is already multiple and contrapuntal. It includes the particular features of a building's architecture; its changing significance over time; the social relations it embodies; as well as potential histories (Azoulay, 2019) that persist and impress on the present through the social fabric, marked by accidental or enforced absence from the official historical register. 'It wasn't intentional', Goebbels (2019: 86) states, 'but it turns out that I am attracted by previously ignored artefacts of the past and the possibility of discovering qualities that have been lost'.

For example, the Kraftzentrale, Landschaftspark Duisburg-Nord afforded multiple resonances with *De Materie* – quite literally, with the chiming staccato chords that reverberated in this vast acoustic space, each decaying perfectly in time for the next. The work's preoccupation with the relationships between matter and spirit, science and religion, nature and culture chime with this site too. This former 'central power plant' and storage depot of the Thyssen foundry and steelworks was also a centre for power, creating the material structures and naval force on which German industry – and military expansion – were built.[35] The three texts of *De Materie*'s first part similarly connects the building of the Dutch nation state (with a section of the 1581 Act of Abjuration, marking Dutch independence from Spanish rule), a treatise on ship-building, and an early atomic theory by the Dutch philosopher and theologian David Gorlaeus. With a structuring contribution from stage and lighting designer Klaus Grünberg – one of his long-standing collaborators – Goebbels' production featured a landscape of six giant, luminescent tent-like structures (Figure 7), warehouses of mercurial light glowing in the dark from which, eventually, emerged

---

[35] Its founder, August Thyssen, as well as being a friend and collector of Rodin's sculptures, was a staunch German nationalist, heavily involved in supporting the First World War effort. His son Fritz, his successor at the war's end, was a fierce opponent of the Versailles settlement and a significant funder of Hitler – to the extent that the Dada artist John Heartfield depicted him as Hitler's puppetmaster.

Figure 7 *De Materie* / Park Avenue Armory. Image courtesy of Heiner Goebbels

a number of figures in what appeared as alien biohazard suits. Not one, but three zeppelins cruised the hall, a faint echo, perhaps, of the miniature motorised zeppelin Cage deployed in the original Frankfurt production of *Europeras 1 & 2*.

These airships may also have inspired the flock of sheep. As well as echoing the narrative of ecological regeneration by re-wilding this post-industrial performance space, the idea had an intuitive logic that Goebbels attributed post hoc – two years after the production – to a childhood experience. His father often took him, aged about seven, to 'a local green airport for gliders', where he would play.

> There were always sheep, and there was always a glider. And I remember that was the first time I met a shepherd. And I asked him what it needed to become a shepherd. He said 'You have to pass a shepherd exam'. And I said, 'What is that?' He answered: 'You have to be able to stand with the crook for an hour [like this]'.[36]

The resonances of this production with the site were not fully determined, a frame through which *De Materie* might be 'read' or understood. The event was not an echo of meanings external to it, congealed in its iron frame. Likewise, this was no rationalisation, psychologisation, or mystical symbolisation. There was no hidden subtext to the flock's appearance, no dog whistle.

---

[36] Interview with the author, 12 October 2018. Goebbels stood up at this point and mimed the action of standing with a crook.

These were not sacrificial lambs, offered as symbols of a greater meaning, and there was no 'good shepherd' to secure the passage of intention. It was, rather, a *felt* rightness – prior to any inscription in memory – that signalled an affirmation, just as free improvisers may find a 'sweet spot', a sense of connection that does not rely on a self-conscious schema or structure.

> I have to trust myself because I'm not trying to build symbols, to find the key for something, the meaning or interpretation in the material. When I chose to work with the sheep, I had no idea why I did that. I only knew that it was an intriguing tension, [this] counterpoint between music, sheep and this assemblage. .... Then people come and interpret it. People very soon came up with their interpretations.

Goebbels selects texts and constructs his own work in similar ways, finding a common link – a framework, 'system of criteria' or restriction – to bring together diverse materials from which he can improvise and compose. It offers a way of forming a consistency and coherence through an 'absent centre', a genus that itself remains unrepresented, un-present. He gives the example of Alain Robbe-Grillet's nouveau roman *La Jalousie* as 'a book about jealousy but [which] never mentions it', offering instead 'all the elements' – showing acts of suspicion, surveillance, obsession – 'without directly expressing any emotions. But by reading you create all the emotions yourself' (Goebbels, 1996). So, for example, the texts of *I Went to the House but Did Not Enter* all deal with hesitation and failure; and notions of the forest linked those of *Ou bien le débarquement désastreux*, prompting Goebbels to deploy only sounds faithful to whatever has to do with wood. 'I'm quite superstitious concerning material. .... All the materials must have their roots around some centre' (Goebbels and Gourgouris, 2004).

What, then, might be the 'absent centre' around which Goebbels approached his curatorial composition of the Ruhrtriennale? That which each of the productions had in common, without itself being represented as a theme or artistic statement, was precisely the post-industrial landscape of the Emscher River, the Ruhr basin, and specifically the spaces in which most of the productions were staged. 'Site', here, is not only a physical entity that pre-conditions what may occur; nor is it reducible to a given history to be recovered and revealed. It is not, as we will discover, a community, culture, or collective identifiable by or inscribed through its relationship to a location or practice. It is, rather, informed by all of these, counterposed as a limited set of possibilities from which a space for improvisation – for something unanticipated – to appear. What appears is precisely something neither determined by nor indebted to the past, but the revelation of a shift in time, a cleft in causation, and the presence of a changing authority.

5.2 Polyphonic and Polychronic Space

> Making music is a social activity, and whoever has once experienced this with
> a degree of pleasure is inclined to marvel at the fact that there could be a decent
> sound under the hierarchical and alienated conditions of hired musicians.
>
> *(Goebbels, 2015: 69)*

These particular spaces had two further characteristics that Goebbels exploited, and that have shaped his own practice. Whilst their industrial past and repurposed present necessarily affected the events they hosted, these nevertheless were relatively neutral – agnostic – as to artistic medium. They had been repurposed as flexible spaces with removable tiered seating and mechanisms for separating off areas through curtained walls. They were not acoustically designed for opera or spoken word, and the stage or display areas were not fixed. Neither white cubes nor black boxes, they were simultaneously self-contained *and* open to the transformation of the meanings they bequeathed. As a consequence, secondly, they did not prescribe a given mode of production. There was no restricted 'get in' time, no limitation of technical infrastructure beyond the cost of a production's installation, and – considering the festival's prestige – no friction with the management of these spaces and their imperatives to generate income and visitor numbers.

> My whole story with performing arts is a story of producing in former
> industrial buildings ... which has a logic in the way I produce, because
> I don't produce in a theatrical rhythm. I don't rehearse in the afternoon for
> a repertoire system. ... I need to have the space for my work. I need to work
> with everything from the very first day, and this isn't possible in repertoire
> theatres. And that was the best way to prepare me for the Ruhrtriennale.[37]

Such 'laboratory conditions' would be a prerequisite for creating genuinely new artistic experiences.[38] Goebbels' first trial with the sheep, to prove the concept could work, took place a year in advance of the performance (indeed his productions often begin with a period of experimentation, three to five days, a year ahead of time). Not trusting to fortune, they would gambol in seven rehearsals prior to the opening night, something almost unthinkable for any conventional performing venue.

The hierarchy of elements – the privileging of text and representational meaning in conventional theatre, of sound and instrumental technique in music, of moving image for narrative film, of the gestalt for early Minimalist

---

[37] Interview with the author, 12 October 2018.

[38] 'What we urgently need in addition to the repertoire theatres are laboratories for theatre and music-theatre, in which *everything* can be called into question. ... Isn't it just like with a car? A new car won't be invented at the assembly line either' (Goebbels, 2015: 80).

sculpture, or the concept for Conceptual Art – is also a corollary of its form of production. Eisler was highly critical of Hollywood practices, for example, that demanded representational music and sound design to reinforce a given sequence, affect, and message, often with a division of labour between composers specialising in military music, sentimental love songs, overtures and intermezzi, Viennese operetta, or jazz (Eisler, 1999: 103). For Goebbels, this is a function of the temporality of production:

> With regards to conventional production methods, in an institutional production of theatre or music theatre anything which comes late in the process is only going to be illustrative; it does not have the power to change anything else which has already been established during the rehearsal period. When the original light is set up in the last three days of a production you can only light what is already there, you cannot change the staging by means of the light anymore.
>
> That is why I work with all elements from the very first moment. I work with light, sound, and amplification. Even when there is no audience I amplify as if there was, because the amplification is a force in itself, sound design is an art form in itself. (Rebstock and Roesner, 2012)

In aiming to avoid creating a fixed hierarchy of means, Goebbels is fundamentally concerned with the *relations between elements*, relations that are constantly changing through time. This was a pivotal lesson he had learned from working in theatre, when a slight change to the music – the rhythm, say, or placement of speakers – made it unrecognisable for a choreographer as the same piece it had been the previous day.

> If it did not have the same effect as the day before, it was not the same music. I suddenly learned – and this has perhaps been the single most significant experience I have had in this profession – how to comprehend the music differently, to shift the criteria, and to hear music not so much internally as with the distance of the scene as a whole. This was an incredibly important experience for me. (Goebbels, 1995)[39]

By shifting the accent of relationships between elements, destabilising and restabilising orders of relation, Goebbels could create a constructive ambiguity within one and the same piece between the experience of a concert, an installation, a performance, a theatre work, and so on. The 'pleasant irritation' this creates of establishing and disrupting expectations enables him to maintain a rhythm of perception that remains open to transformation and metamorphosis, to a work's strange deviation (Goebbels, 2008; 2015: 88).

---

[39] Eisler gives a remarkably similar account of an occasion working with Brecht (Eisler, 1975/ 2014: 71).

The paradox of this approach, whose fundamental goal is to adopt an openness to becoming otherwise, is that – unlike with Cage – nothing is left to chance. Where Cage crafted open situations precisely to avoid any and all dependent relations between elements, Goebbels and his collaborators meticulously compose these relations, allowing them to constantly mutate and shift, like different 'voices' taking turns to carry the subject of a fugue. This method is exacting, precise, and emphasises the social dimension of production in the collective responsibility among equals tasked with different specialisms. Goebbels insists on working from the strength of each rather than by dictating or directing 'from the top', and brought in several of his regular production team to the Ruhrtriennale to ensure this.

> The respect for the other, trusting his perspective and his competence, also ties in with refraining from the dominance of one discipline, and the openness to an aesthetic coexistence based on heterogeneity. . . . To see one's own lack of competency not as a weakness to be downplayed, but to use it as a strength in order to enrich one's artistic perspective with the perspective of the other – that is the core of working collectively. (Goebbels, 2015: 90)[40]

It also has a musical dimension – a compositional principle for achieving the simultaneous independence *and* interdependence of elements without a model, primary form, hierarchy, or centre – providing the principle of this mode of production:

> I definitely went through the school of Bach. Polyphonics is my basic music experience from the beginning, when I started. I play piano, and I started at the age of five, and I'm sure by the age of six I started playing Bach and I haven't stopped. This independency or the relationship of two, three, four voices, is probably something that gives me the biggest pleasure, that I try to translate into the other mediums. . . . *and as part of the relations it's important that the centre isn't occupied.* When I play Bach – and I play him every day – I play fugue differently every day because I fill it up with different emotions, questions, and curiosities for new relations. It's endless. It's pretty empty the piece itself, but you can fill it up with many options. And this is what I hope is going to happen with my work as well.[41]

Within his Ruhrtriennale programmes, this form of organisation – this rhythm of stability and instability articulated in the relationship between

---

[40] See also Rebstock and Roesner (2012): 'The biggest advantage of working with the same team since ten, fifteen, twenty years ago is: you don't have to speak. You speak a lot in advance and hopefully come up with clever and intelligent concepts, but it's very important that you have the space and the option and the confidence in the team to react and create directly without explaining [. . .] a much more pleasant and open way, more open to inspirations for everybody, than the hysterical silence in the authoritarian way of directing.'

[41] Interview with the author, 12 October 2018. Emphasis added.

elements – operated primarily at the level of the staged encounter, rather than in the abstract 'view from above' that might analyse or treat the festival's constellation of events as a fixed score.[42] All the same, the flow of events had a rhythm shifting the accent between artists entering this hybrid terrain from different specialisms, between different modes of attention and structures of event (performance, installation, discussion, and so on), and offering resonances in the spaces between disparate works. For example, Anne Teresa de Keersmaeker's exquisite choreography to Schoenberg's *Verklärte Nacht* ('Transfigured Night') illumined the 'night concert' production of Morton Feldman's *For Philip Guston*, also on 16 August 2014, running from 11 pm until half past 3 am the next morning. The massive piles and clouds of bovine 'bone dust' – thirty tonnes of death's fertiliser – that animated theatre director Romeo Castellucci's brutal performing installation to Stravinsky's *Sacre du Printemps* provided a similar counterpoint to the animated production of *De Materie* with which it ran concurrently.[43]

However, perhaps the most direct and dramatic expression of this contrapuntal method came with the technology developed for Goebbels' *Stifters Dinge* (re-presented at the Ruhrtriennale in 2013), a 'performative installation' or 'no-man theatre', with neither actors nor musicians. Instead, his colleague and friend Hubert Machnik (who later worked on Castellucci's *Sacre*) developed a Max MSP interface attached to a music keyboard from which Goebbels 'could control nearly everything in a musical way' (Rebstock and Roesner, 2012), from producing wooden and metallic sounds in the set, bass sounds on tubes, and scratching sounds by moving stones, to controlling lights, and so on.

Commissioned by Artangel and first presented in London at Ambika P3, 2008, *Stifters Dinge* (Figure 8) is also exemplary for the aesthetic principle on which this emphasis on an openness to alterity is based. The work is ostensibly the same for every performance. Coded into a technical network controlling all aspects, monitored from a desk behind the audience, and with only the barest involvement of two overalled stage assistants for the opening sequence

---

[42] It is notable that Goebbels' productions typically 'begin' before the audience enters the auditorium, eschew an interval that would break focus and concentration, and their endings are often similarly ambiguous, opening onto the time and space of their own surroundings – as for example at Mayfield, Manchester for *Everything that happened and would happen* (2018), where the audience's exit from the space was marked as an extension and continuation of the performance.

[43] 'I synthesized the notion of sacrifice in a very modern and reduced thought by referring to the industrial oblivion to which sacrifice has been condemned. [...] The bone dust refers to an industrial notion of sacrifice. Here we remember the animals that by the thousands are led to the slaughter bank without any sacrificial ritual, without any accounting for their death' (Castellucci, 2014).

Figure 8 *Stifters Dinge.* Wonge Bergmann / Ruhrtriennale. Image courtesy of Heiner Goebbels

(who soon depart), the piece is almost completely automated. At the same time, the experience is different on each occasion. What changes each night, of course, is the audience: the 'space of appearance' or, as Goebbels put it, the 'space of the Other' (Matthews, 2019). 'Based on Hannah Arendt you can consider every performance to be a "public sphere, . . . in which it is necessary not to attack each other" – neither in the work relations nor in the relation to the audience' (Goebbels, 2015: 58, 44). The threat of violence is present or implicit, Arendt shows, when authority is external to its being exercised. I now turn to her work to grasp how authority – and therefore value – might be understood to emerge immanently from the public encounter, avoiding the twin catastrophes that Goehr notes of either foregoing it altogether through a resigned relativism or reimposing it as another external principle by fiat. This requires paying particular attention to the careful distinctions Arendt makes between the private and public spheres, and between the articulated movements that comprise 'action'. I begin, however, with the very musical matter of the inclinations of time that shape experience.

5.3 Potential Publics

> This small non-time-space in the very heart of time, unlike the world and the culture into which we are born, can only be indicated, but cannot be inherited and handed down from the past; each new generation . . . must discover and ploddingly pave it anew. *(Arendt, 1961: 13)*

> Without this transcendence into a potential earthly immortality, no politics, strictly speaking, no common world and no public realm, is possible. *(Arendt, 1998: 55)*

In *The Human Condition*, Arendt describes two contradictory principles that mark out the human condition.[44] The first is a self-consciousness of our own mortality, and so of the futility of existence, presaging a desire for *im*mortality, to defy death or at least to leave an enduring mark. The second is our paradoxical capacity – our freedom in the fullest sense – to affect our relation to time, to alter the course of our own being, and so to depart from any notion of human 'essence' or foundation external to the individual. The human condition involves the constant production and metamorphosis of 'human nature', manifest in the accomplishment of individuation. The individual is not, here, a representative of the species as a given and unalterable condition. Each person is essentially unique, a new creation unlike any other before or to come, a quality Arendt called 'natality'. We *differ*. The collective cannot, then, be bound, ordered, or governed by an external or prior identity – of nationality, ethnicity, gender – not even of 'the human' as a species. Its identity is constituted by the very difference of its members, its fundamental negativity. Arendt calls this public as such a *plurality*.

---

[44] It is important to note that Arendt does not present this schematically, implying an anthropocentric metaphysics. Her approach is, rather, traced historically, in particular through a history of Western philosophy. 'Not the capabilities of man, but the constellation which orders their mutual relationships can and does change historically. Such changes can best be observed in the changing self-interpretations of man throughout history' (Arendt, 1998: 62). The account given here is intended as a heuristic model to give a more concise structural framework within which Goebbels' musical and theatrical approach might be understood.

The desire to last and the ability to begin anew are forces in tension that articulate the field of human experience and its cultural expression.

Arendt notes that in contrast to the distinctions between 'productive' and 'unproductive' labour, 'skilled' or 'unskilled' work, and finally 'manual' or 'intellectual' labour – which only qualify a singular idea of action – Greek and Latin had two words that mark an essential division. The first term (*arkhē*, *agere*) indicated a beginning, a setting in motion or initiation: a formal or efficient cause. The second (*prattein*, *gerere*) was a passing through, achieving, bearing, or finishing. The ability to lead, to create, to set off, is a capacity of the individual. The power to accomplish, however, lies in the *potential* of the public: its potency lasts only for the duration of its gathering, and disappears with its dispersal. (Arendt notes the derivation of 'power' from *potentia*, as also the German *Macht* from *mögen*, not from *machen*.) Enduring fame is not in the exclusive gift of history's 'authors'.

It is the relation between these two forms of possibility that define Arendt's three paradigms of agency – the vita activa – each with its own rhythm.

'Labour' describes the repetitive, cyclical tasks of sustaining life: of eating, sleeping, reproduction, providing, and resting. Barely differentiated from other species let alone from each other, this survival mode of being is characterised by the rapid consumption of its own production, and so by implication extends to other aspects of culture whose concern with the body is less immediately apparent, such as entertainment (understood as a disposable form of recuperation, preparing the individual for further labour).

Labour neither initiates nor endures. It is essentially marked by privation, categorically excluded from a *public* world that would be free from the submission to natural necessity, and so located in the 'private' domain of the household. Its bare existence can only be redeemed by a different mode of being: work.

Work is defined by acts of making objects, of reifying, fabricating, and authoring things that may persist beyond the life cycle and daily necessity, and so providing a semblance of stability, a dwelling (marking a 'surplus' to labour that Marx considered constitutive of capitalist relations). The human capacity to act on nature, to qualify and master it, giving it a new purpose – what the Greeks called *tekhnē* – is fundamental to work. Indeed, this quality of means–end rationality, of planning, calculation and strategy, gives it a distinct beginning – in a judgement, decision, usually as an image, idea, or concept – and an end product. It defines the vector, the trajectory of a line, a line that can be repeated, re-drawn. If a table, say – or a trombone, or conventionally notated composition, a work – is damaged, destroyed, or just badly performed, it can be re-made without losing its essential identity.

This making takes place *prior* to its public life, before the object enters the world of market relations in which it gains value through exchange, prior to its curation in the conventional sense. For 'value is the quality a thing can never possess in privacy but acquires automatically the moment it appears in public' (Arendt, 1998: 164). *Homo faber* invents, but this natality is separated from the public domain on which its value depends. The durability of its objects is conditional on their continued utility. In a world of exchangeable values, worked 'objects' are subject to deflation, to being forgotten, passed over, neglected. Musical works can both enter and quietly depart the canon.

Only in Arendt's third paradigm are these two possibilities – of casting off and sailing through to landing safely – and their respective forms of agency linked as one distinct movement.

It is only through 'action' as such that both the new can be initiated *and* a durable world outlasting the individual may be salvaged. Unlike labour and work, action's value is neither immediately consumed nor external and derivative, but immanent to its own movement, inspiring by its own exemplar. Actions call for *remembrance*, a reconciliation with mortality that preserves through collective memory – carried in ritual, commemorated in song, recorded ('taken back into the heart', the *cor*) or otherwise 'burned into the heart' (*cor-urat*) – to borrow Varro's curatorial etymology (Hamilton, 2013: 74). Without care – without curation – we merely stem an inevitable erasure by time. Even monuments, even palaces of industry, are left to decay, ruination, and dust. Significantly, then, cultural practices of recollection and cherishing cannot be compelled from without, for even duties of repetition – the obligatory singing of national anthems, say, or the rote incantation of prayer – lose their meaning without heartfelt commitment.

The distinction and co-dependence of the two dimensions of action make it both irreversible and unpredictable. No two actions – no two performances of *Stifters Dinge*, however automated – will be identical. The same process of initiation will always be carried through with unrepeatable consequences. Action has a quality of the miraculous, then, not least because the leading gesture acquires its recognition – its *authority* – only retrospectively through the power of the plurality to transform it. 'The new occurs against the backdrop of statistical laws, of means and probabilities – always in the guise of a miracle' (Arendt, 1998: 178).

Two fundamental principles defined by a lack: a world that endures only in the individual's absence; and a common world that is shaped without being made, forced, or intended.

Arendt traces these paradoxes in the movements of (Western) history, for the space of appearance has no inevitability and no essential foundation. They saturate the antinomies of culture and nature, mind and body, individual and collective, memory and history; and they articulate the political field, as well as its relation to art.

One of the tragedies of this human condition has been the repeated attempts to overcome the precarity, vulnerability, and uncertainty of the process of leading and instantiating by bracketing the power of the plurality (to determine its outcome). The sovereign, for example, works 'the people', moulding them according to his idea; nation states, like the Dutch, simply transferred this sovereign identity to their lawfully recognised citizens, as the *Act of Abjuration* describes. Plato provided a paradigm in his 'philosopher-king' of *The Republic*. Guarding against 'mob rule' in the wake of Socrates' trial and death, he sought models of authority between ruler and ruled, in which compulsion might not appear dependent on external legitimacy but rather be immanent to the relation (akin to the prior principle of self-mastery) – such as those of a master and his slaves, physician and patient, a helmsman and the ship's passengers, or between a shepherd and his sheep. In each instance, expertise *dominates* and commands; indeed, Foucault (2009) emphasises precisely the role of the 'pastorate' paradigm in the emergence of 'governmentality', the articulation of modern subjects habituated to being led even in the absence of explicit instruction. Granting power and the right to violence exclusively to the judgement, idea, scheme, or work *prior* to any potential of the plurality in this way defines a mode of politics without the freedom proper to public life.

By contrast, for Arendt, it is only because of the capacity of *each* individual to craft a world anew, paradoxically, that a common political realm as such can be understood. Freedom – the potential for all to differ – becomes *the* political issue. 'To *be* free and to act are the same' (Arendt, 1961: 153, also 146). This fundamentally shifts the question of artistic autonomy and its relation to politics and the public sphere. In contrast with a notion of craft production that determines value in advance of its public appearance, marking a clear distinction from politics, the performance arts – or rather, the performativity of art – are themselves implicitly political.

> Only where things can be seen by many in a variety of aspects without changing their identity, so that those who are gathered around them know they see sameness in utter diversity, can worldly reality truly and reliably appear. (Arendt, 1998: 57)

An action open to the unpredictability of its effects within a plurality, requiring the presence of a public, an audience, has a distinct affinity with theatre as an opening into the miraculous, the unforeseeable. Indeed, this process can only be objectified through a form of repetition, through a *mimesis* of action presented through drama.

> This is also why the theater is the political art par excellence; only there is the political sphere of human life transposed into art. By the same token, it is the only art whose sole subject is man in his relationship to others.
>
> (Arendt, 1998: 188)

By this account, art is not autonomous from the public domain, but constitutes a political realm of its own. Aesthetics and ethics intertwine. Art's autonomy is *not* intrinsic but predicated on a specific relation to public life distinguished from modes of human activity based either on bare existence or on forms of making severed from or superimposed on their public appearance. It would, in particular, necessitate a difference from methods of manipulation or control, of imposing conformity or manufacturing consent – or of insisting on an interpretation of an artistic experience predicated on the work-concept and an author-composer.

Whilst there are important differences in Goebbels' work, especially considering the use of language and the phenomenology of the public encounter, this discursion nevertheless illuminates significant features of his curatorial compositional method.

The plurality of audiences – its internal diversity – has been totemic for Goebbels. Not only has he consistently and deliberately brought together audiences for different types of art and performance – literature, theatre, dance, pop, post-punk, concert music, opera – but he has also changed his approach when he felt the audiences his activity attracted became too homogenous.

> I think this is also one of the reasons why I stopped Cassiber, because I saw that the audience was becoming a kind of scene, predictable, . . . I tried rather – and this was what I considered a challenge for me – to seduce a new audience. You see, the problem is that I don't belong to any scene. I don't belong to the contemporary composer scene, nor do I belong to the theatre director scene.
>
> (Warburton and Livingston, 1997)

Not content to take the aerial view of market segmentation, he insisted on 'meet[ing] the audience on an eye level', an approach detailed down to the level of grammar. 'One of the first statements I gave [to the team], I said "please let's not use imperatives"'.[45] Goebbels' statements in the festival brochures, as well as his video trailers, accordingly expressed confidence in potential audiences and their curiosity towards the unknown through an open invitation. For example: 'You make a great impression on everyone with your curiosity, openness, artistic daring and the directness of your response. . . . I thank you

---

[45] Interview with the author. The principle of operating on an equal footing applied also to his working relationship with Lukas Crepaz, then the Ruhrtriennale's Managing Director, whereby 'responsibility was completely shared 50:50 [. . .], signing every contract etc. That's changed completely now'.

for having accepted this subjectively chosen programme and for continuing to accept it' (Goebbels, 2014). There was no 'hard sell'; connection was paramount. In interviews, he commonly cites a lesson learned from Eisler, of 'Fortschritt und Zurücknahme' (progress and recuperation): that confronting people with work that deliberately negates past models, that is uncompromisingly avant-garde without retaining or offering other elements that provide a degree of familiarity – and pleasure, welcoming emotional responses – is counterproductive (Till, 2002). The tension between complexity and simplicity is key to his work. The seductive qualities of the material he uses counterbalances the work's unpredictability, a principle he carried through in his selection of events for the Ruhrtriennale. Despite the absence of repertoire pieces and an emphasis on new and commissioned productions, then, people flocked to the festival, which achieved its best ever attendances.

Three aspects of the festival in particular deserve special mention, and receive it in Goebbels' introductions: the involvement of local people within productions by international artists and curators; the No Education programme; and his treatment of politics.

In his first year alone, for example, he emphasised the involvement of 'experts, young professionals and laymen from the Ruhr' as assistants in Cage's *Europeras 1 & 2*, as performers in Lemi Ponifasio's production of Carl Orff's *Prometheus*, as *FOLK* in Castellucci's work, as dancers for the Nature Theater of Oklahoma's 'off-off musical', as performers in *12 Rooms*, and as drummers with The Boredoms.

Nowhere was this principle of *producing* a political community more apparent than in the No Education initiative, which took pride of place as the first part of the programme detailed in the brochures, prior to any specific events. This was no pedagogical 'offshoot' of the 'main programme', but quite literally front and centre. Young people embodied a principle of curiosity that was both encouraged and offered as a model for all other audiences and participants: 'Children can show us the way by reacquainting us with abilities we forgot we had, so they also take the lead in our *No Education* projects'. This would be uncompromising, as curator and dramaturg Marietta Piekenbrock pointed out: 'There is no reason to protect spectators from complexity, no matter how young they might be' (Goebbels, 2012: 12).[46]

An openness to the encounter was the priority. Expertise conferred no prior authority or privilege:

> The performances of the Ruhrtriennale are chosen to promote an interaction among music, theater, dance, performance, video, and architecture with no

---

[46] These positions are amplified in Goebbels' 'Nine Theses on the future of an education for the performing arts' (Goebbels, 2015: 77–81).

education or prior knowledge. . . . *No Education* projects do not seek to obtain any result, instead postulating that a solution is not always required.

This process extended to inviting a 'jury' of young people to review the festival, including ones that subjected Goebbels himself and his guest artists to critique. Developed with the Canadian group Mammalian Diving Reflex – whose approach emphasises intuitive responses rather than strategy and pre-planning – the Children's Choice Awards gave a mixed group of twelve- to fourteen-year-olds VIP access to the entire programme (including the most expensive front row seats).[47]

Where 'political' issues were raised in the programme, through forums each year in conjunction with the newspaper *Die Zeit*, they emerged from the experience of the programme, not as themes that dictated it. So, for example, Daniel Cohn-Bendit spoke on the crisis in Europe on the last day of the production of Cage's *Europeras 1 & 2*. A discussion on 'Global Co-operation in the 21st Century' similarly explored forms of unconscious or unintended mutual influence and collaboration in 2013, within a programme emphasising artistic partnerships, exemplified on the same day by Massive Attack and documentary-maker Adam Curtis' exposition of globalised power's impover- ishing attempts to control the destinies of societies.

The forums held in Goebbels' final year – on the political values of *not* knowing in advance, and on 'The Gift of Co-operation', exploring forms of mutual indebtedness and global solidarity – were less clearly linked to individ- ual events than they were emblematic of his reconfiguring of political space itself. Politics is not a separate field, here, a representational form, but active as a form of co-production following the path set out by Eisler – also echoing Benjamin's 'The Author As Producer' (1998) – and consistent with Arendt's transfiguring public realm. Indeed, this was a *musical* revelation that had set him on his path:

> Listening to Eisler changed my life. His work conveyed to me that there is a way in which music and politics can be linked, not by forming one layer upon another but by incorporating the political within the musical material.
> (Goebbels and Gourgouris, 2004)

---

[47] 'They created their own categories, like "The Performance That Bored Me To Sleep." And someone like Bob Wilson got the prize for "The slowest show," and Anna Teresa de Keersmaeker got the award for "The piece I'd most like to leave soonest," or something like that. Everyone had to accept it.' Interview with the author. Goebbels himself was awarded, variously: 'The Worst Costumes' (for *Delusion of the Fury*); 'I want that thing!' and 'The show where I thought wtf?!' (for *Stifter's Dinge*); 'The Girliest Show' (for *When the Mountain changed its clothing*); and 'Best Drama' (for *Europeras 1 & 2*) – all proudly listed with his other honorary notices: www.heinergoebbels.com/en/about/ awards_honors, accessed 27 October 2020.

Music was never 'only music', but always also a *gesture* – a public act. This did not need to address politics by commenting on it, as if it were separate; its enactment was already political. A politics defined by uncoupling the act of initiating, of strategy, from its public actualisation, and re-attaching the latter to the former, could only court disaster. This is a moral Goebbels also drew from Heiner Müller, who insisted that political art was 'like harnessing a horse to a car. The car doesn't run well and the horse doesn't survive it either' (Goebbels and Gourgouris, 2004; Barker, 2010). Instead, 'once you're working in an open-minded way, I trust that sooner or later the work will come to breathe in the situation around it'. The world 'outside' the performance space seems to bear an uncanny resemblance to what has been encountered 'inside'. Reality is only as strange as fiction.

Goebbels recounts an exemplary instance from the production of his opera – or scenic concert – *Landscape with Distant Relatives,* in which, following a photographic work by the Albanian artist Sisley Xhafa, he presented the Ensemble Modern 'wearing black hoods, of the kind we know from bank robberies' (Figure 9). Whilst on stage in Geneva, television screens at home were showing Chechen rebels wearing identical masks, taking hostages in a Moscow theatre, and the training of the Russian armed forces preparing to storm the theatre, also wearing the same headgear (Goebbels, 2015: 15–16).

If the political in Goebbels' curatorial and musical-artistic work is not a matter of representation, then it is decisively one of enactment. For Arendt, this requires a public sphere in which each individual is equally capable of difference, and so free to act. This is far from self-evident, of course, with audiences at performances: does each member independently form their own impression and interpretation, is there a unified and collective experience, or might there be other ways in which a plurality might express the emergence of a meaningful – and thus authoritative – encounter? The pastoral scene from *De Materie* can be helpful once more both in considering Goebbels' approach to audiences and to what this enchanted gathering might share with us of the effect of wonder.

5.4 The Animals That Therefore We Are

> When our attempts to classify what we have seen no longer apply is when things start to get interesting. . . . Perhaps you will find your own terms . . . or you'll simply enjoy the fact that we have been rendered speechless. *(Goebbels, 2014)*

This was not Goebbels' only attempt to work with wildlife. He impishly recounts a poker game of pitching concepts for an earlier work based on texts by Elias Canetti – which became *Eraritjaritjaka* – to the artistic director of the

Figure 9 *Landscape with Distant Relatives.* Wonge Bergmann / Ensemble Modern. Image courtesy of Heiner Goebbels

Théâtre Vidy de Lausanne (his regular production partner between 1998 and 2012). After failing to register interest with his first ideas he raised the stakes by proposing to cast an animal, 'another non-manufactured dynamic thing with a reality of its own, to which the texts could react'. He suggested a heron, though this proved too difficult: 'unpredictable, too expensive and problematic for an international tour because of baffling heron-entry-regulations' (Goebbels, 2015: 22). An eagle owl too proved unsatisfactory, so they settled on a 'robotic' creature, comprising two lights, remotely controlled, on wheels (Figure 10).

Goebbels' video installation in Dresden – named after Canetti's *The Human Province* – featured material from *Eraritjaritjaka* alongside its companion piece based on the sequence with the flock from *De Materie*, implying an affinity between them.[48] They worry the hard distinction of culture and nature, corresponding with and supplementing Andriessen's exploration of the dialectic of spirit and matter, mind and world. Exploring the potential for wonder in this relation of human and animal, a further connection emerges with Adalbert Stifter, the nineteenth-century Austrian writer and painter known for his precise and otherworldly accounts of encountering nature. A short text of his featured in

---

[48] Goebbels described the video of the sheep as a 'non-human province', and so in dialectical relation with the installation from *Eraritjaka*. Email to the author, 12 March 2016.

Figure 10 *Eraritjaritjaka*.L. Sch. Image courtesy of Heiner Goebbels

De Materie's programme book, and Goebbels noted the correlation of his staging of it with *Stifters Dinge*: both empty the stage of human performers in preference for dynamic – animate and automated – realities of their own.[49] Texts by Canetti and Stifter therefore guide my reflection on this scene and its resonances for Goebbels' method of curatorial composing, not by asking what the sheep might represent but in considering what they do, or more specifically the dynamic effect they introduce.

---

[49] https://bit.ly/36L8rLW, accessed 29 October 2020.

To begin with, Goebbels does not domesticate this Other or present us with a fabled animal with which we might identify but presents us with a puzzle of our own making. What might the sheep mean for us, or what do they want of us? Are they watching and listening to us just as we observe and attend to them? Rilke considered this gaze in his *Duino Elegies*:

> *and the sly animals see at once*
> *how little at home we are*
> *in the interpreted world.* (Rilke, 2000: 5)

His beasts unburden their gaze on us, leaving us unsettled, nomadic. The sheep here likewise regard us, the hearing herd, in our serene ignorance. They are uncorralled, unconcerned at our ruminations, our woolly thinking and knit brows. They are not sacrificial offerings to our Adamic capacities for naming and explaining; the dissections of our linguistic abstractions leaves them indifferent. They are significantly there but do not signify, suspending any closure (and disbelief) in simple comprehension and so allowing the feeling of time to drift without need for resolution – just as the harmonic oscillations of chiming percussion pause the sense of momentum and rhythmic propulsion of the previous scene. Their astonishing entry introduces the feeling of an enigma, an opening to an effect of symbolisation prior to any specific meaning. Writing of this effect in *Stifters Dinge*, Goebbels claims:

> We are powerless against other things, strange things; this is where our sense of time no longer takes effect: here, we are forced to accept a completely different kind of time . . . you could call it, perhaps a bit loftily, 'the time of the other'. (Goebbels, 2015: 32)

Going further, how is this passage of unresolved appearance inflected by the fact that we are presented not with one animal but a multitude? In contrast with Derrida (2002), who teased the question of the human animal and its ambivalent dialectic through the emergence of the autobiographical subject – the 'I am' – Goebbels invites us to encounter this plurality of beings collectively: 'we are'. Moving to this slow dance, this pavane, might this troupe be considered a metamorphosis of the Greek chorus, somehow standing as our on-stage proxies? As an audience, do we share a 'herd mentality', or is this relationship between the individual and the collective a fundamental aspect of what is given us to behold? Might this be the way a plurality makes sense? The scene encourages us to consider this bucolic ochlocracy, this mob polity, as a metaphor – or rather, a 'crowd symbol' in Canetti's term – for ourselves. Do we want to be shepherded, told what to expect, or do we each insist on the freedom to form our own interpretation? Where does meaning arise, between the individual – the sheep – and the collective – the sheep?

On 15 July 1927, Canetti found himself a participant in an uprising, a revolutionary dynamic of a populous that burned down Vienna's Palace of Justice. A 'just verdict' had been proclaimed in the acquittal of paramilitaries responsible for murdering protesting workers, and a spontaneous movement formed in response. Police fired on the people, killing more than 600.

Crowds and Power became the outcome of his lifelong fascination with this mass phenomenon that felt neither voluntary nor involuntary: 'It seems as if the movement of some of [the crowd] transmits itself to the others. But that is not all; they have a goal, which is there *before they can find words for it*' (Canetti, 1973: 16 – emphasis added). As no single account of this enigmatic experience was available, his search ranged across diverse literatures, from philosophies (both Western and Eastern) and anthropology to natural history. 'I read Darwin, hoping to learn something about the formation of crowds among animals, and I thoroughly perused books on insect societies' (Canetti, 1982: 253).[50]

The crowd as such forms (like the sheep before us) prior to representation as a tendency already in motion before the individual's entry into language. It has – again – no essence, core, or origin. Its identity – its branding – can only be impressed from outside. At the same time, there is a purposiveness to its movement, a murmuration, a sense of shape.

Canetti approaches this mutable body from the question of the fear of touching, as posed by Freud (Malabou, 2015). In contrast with the psychoanalyst – who saw the experience of 'the mass', the pressing of bodies, as a relief from the burden of individuation which could then be transferred to the body of a collective subject – Canetti interposes another possibility. Between an identity with the social and the identity of the individual lies the potential to differ – in Arendt's terms, the transformative power of a plurality. 'What happens to you when you are in the mass is a drastic and enigmatic modification of consciousness' (Malabou, 2015: 29).

Crowds require a sense of direction, he observed, but they can also become 'stagnant' whilst awaiting this vector. Canetti offers theatre and concert audiences as exemplars of a pacified version of such a gathering, sitting 'like a well-drilled herd, still and infinitely patient'.

> The contrast between the stillness of the listeners and the din of the apparatus inflicting itself on them is even more striking in *concerts*. Here everything

---

[50] The importance of observing animals for human collectives became emblematic in *Crowds and Power* – see, for example, the section on *Rhythm* (34–38).

depends on the audience being completely undisturbed. [. . .] People sit there motionless, as though they managed to hear *nothing*. It is obvious that a long and artificial training in stagnation has been necessary here. . . . People who allow music to affect them in a natural way behave quite differently.

(Canetti, 1973: 40)

A 'tranquil' or 'expectation pack', by contrast, 'appears wherever the goal of the pack is one which is not attainable by rapid and intense activity. . . . They aim at something remote, which *cannot* be present for some time'. Such a patient expectation and stillness is emblematic, Canetti suggests, of 'those religions which profess belief in another world' (Canetti, 1973: 135). This superstitious feeling of a necessary yet inchoate demand, motivation or meaning – a purposiveness without purpose perhaps, to invoke Kant's aesthetic formula for 'the Beautiful' – is something to which I will return.

In contrast to the 'closed crowd' that accepts and defends the borders of its identity, the 'open' crowd's capacity to receive and to donate form and shape – its *plasticity*, to use Malabou's (2005) key concept – emerges from the feeling of equality. Each member can *differ equally and mutually* in a rhythm of attraction and alteration, a movement that Canetti explores through the use of masks. 'The mass is the place of a mutual metamorphosis – all its members identifying with each other – and of a masked separation by which those members make themselves unrecognizable' (Malabou, 2015: 33). In contrast with a 'visual mask' by which individuals group under a principle of anonymous identity – an identity not belonging to any single member – an 'acoustic mask' might best be understood as the differential voice of a crowd. Rather than an order of harmony determined by a fundamental tone, it gives a massed gathering a quality of noise, like traffic or surf that moves in waves. That surges and swells. Canetti describes this mask through the Babelesque analogy of

arriv[ing] in a country knowing nothing of the language ... The less one understands the more one imagines. [. . .] Every completely unknown language is a kind of acoustic mask; as soon as one learns it, it becomes a *face*, under-standable and soon familiar. (Canetti, 1973: 435; also Canetti, 1982: 220–1)

It is here, in this animated dynamic between an image of the crowd, of the animals that we are, and a mutable aurality, not yet a common language, that a sense of wonder and symbolic necessity can be encountered. Malabou (2013) explores this astonishment as a *meaningful feeling* precisely in the temporal gap between undifferentiated unself-consciousness and awareness of difference or symbolic otherness within the self. This movement of difference within identity is not a self-feeling (autoaffection) nor yet a 'self' that is feeling (heteroaffection), but a felt emergent power of becoming otherwise, of natality in Arendt's terms. Drawing on book 1 of Aristotle's *Metaphysics*, Malabou states: 'wonder may be seen as the structure of autoaffection: the subject touching itself as if it were a surprising other. Wonder is the philosophical affect as such ... the faculty of self-surprising, the amazement of the mind at itself, its own opening to objects' (Malabou, 2015: 10). Neither involuntary nor intentional, wonder inspires action: 'feelings in general, and wonder in particular, lay the foundations for care, the care of ourselves, the care for ourselves' (51). In addition, perhaps wonder is the curatorial affect as such.

Malabou shows, following Spinoza, that wonder is attracted to singularity, to the new, that which surprises or sticks out and so provokes interest. 'Difficulty' is revealed not as complexity but as a difference from the predictable, the routine, and the facile. It 'reveals to us the beauty of difficult things and attunes our mind to their scarcity and rarity. . . . Wonder is the call of being, the tendency to turn the *conatus* [the affective attunement to life, as a capacity prior to self-production] toward the ontological beauty of the necessity of things' (Malabou, 2013: 41).

Staging this affective capacity of 'things' to puzzle, to mystify, and awe is a feature of Goebbels' practice and typical of many artists he presented at the Ruhrtriennale. It is also indicative of Stifter's writing as his text in *De Materie*'s programme makes clear:

> We call [the world] the greatest wonder. But on the things of the world there is an even greater miracle: life. We stand before the abyss of this riddle in astonishment and impotence. Life touches us so deeply and graciously that everything in which we are able to discover it is related, and everything in which we cannot see it is alien, that we lovingly follow its signs in mosses, herbs, trees, animals, that we eagerly absorb them in the history of the human race and in the representations of individual people, that we poetise life in our arts, and that we are unable to think of ourselves without life. (Ruhrtriennale, 2014)

Moreover, it is not only the 'thingness' of things that matters to Goebbels, it is the *aural* relationship that it presents to an audience, that it speaks – it bleats – in a language of its own:

> we can never be sure with the sounds, the sounds of things because they have their own secret life. They do not have our flesh and blood. We never know what to expect next. They represent the other world, which we cannot master.
> (Goebbels, 2017: 93)

The sounds of things inspire wonder, yet Goebbels does not retreat from language. In his practice, texts provide a counterpoint that 'react' in juxtaposition with 'non-manufactured dynamic thing[s] with a reality of [their] own'. They remain independent, suggestively intertwining with other elements in the composition without framing or overdetermining them. To achieve this effect, Goebbels often separates the speaker from the text, such that words are not enunciated as speech acts (Austin, 1962). They are not performative, world-making, and they are not delivered as opinions, views, or other expressions of inner feelings or thoughts. For example, he routinely invites non-actors, especially musicians, to deliver texts to invite their idiosyncrasies or imperfections to stick out, rub against, or otherwise inflect the self-presence of the language. Likewise, he commonly incorporates multiple languages in the same piece, offering a surplus of the sonic over semantic content: alongside German, English, and French, these have included Mandingo, Arabic, and titles from Japanese and Aboriginal languages. Above all, as noted earlier in his use of 'placeholder texts' to act as an 'absent centre' in the process of production, he draws out the manifest structure of a passage as the level at which meaning is produced in performance (Goebbels, 1996/2002, 1997/2002; Goebbels and Gourgouris, 2004). This could, for example, be at the level of syntax, punctuation, or even in its appearance on the page.[51] Goebbels cites the case of composing music for a production of Georg Buechner's *Dantons Tod*, using a computer to reveal and visualise its poetic structures 'by simply dividing lines at their punctuation marks, emphasising sequences, etc. Following Buechner who once said that "every comma is a stroke of a sabre and every full stop is a head cut off," I later attempted to make the punctuation audible'. Both emphasising the *sounds* of a text and focusing on its structure rather than its semantic content, he invites audiences to worry less about trying to understand the given meaning and instead to listen in to – *and be affected by* – its potential meaning in the encounter.

This potential arises from the *non-connection* of elements, Goebbels claims, a quality he finds also in Canetti's writings and brought out in *Eraritjaritjaka*:

> Maybe it is the connection between the societal, the public and the obstinately self-referential that pervades Canetti's notes as well as the music. ... And maybe a kind of music like Bach's fugal construction, which makes its architecture so transparent, is particularly appropriate for incorporating text as an additional voice. (Goebbels, 2015: 21)

Within this state of calm expectancy, attuned to the emergence of the new as an opening into 'symbolic necessity' – the *feeling* that an image, a gesture, a sound, a phrase *must* be meaningful – wonder has the power to incline us to a sense of being not bound by mortality. Malabou (2016) develops this again in

---

[51] Eisler (1975/2014: 55) gives a remarkably similar account: 'I told Brecht that Shakespeare's punctuation in the first quarto edition isn't in accordance with grammatical rules, but is gestic. This means that the punctuation [. . .] wasn't set according to grammatical rules but followed the raising and lowering of the voices.'

dialogue with Spinoza, reflecting on the encounter with meaning, with a sense of authority. The human tendency to desire closure in (self-)identity, in making an intelligible and so orderly world, disposes us to overinterpreting, to rush to find sense. By withholding the attachment of words to worldly matters – of signifiers to referents, of 'sheep' to sentient beings – meaning could emerge, suspended, through the signified, 'the stable component of a word' – the *thingness* of language, we might say.

> The sacred can become profane because it has no referent and no semantic stability either. In a certain sense, it is a void signified, a *floating signified*, materialized only by transient signifiers: stones (the tablets of the Law), light, fire, a house, a voice, a wind, or a breath. (Malabou, 2016: 104)

Malabou relates Spinoza's argument through the question of Biblical interpretation. As pure text, God's Word would always be open to dispute not least as Hebrew was a lost – or at least highly contested – language, but nor could its truth lie in some transcendental space 'outside' the text. The event of revelation, he claimed, must therefore arise from an attachment of the yearning for the sacred – of a desire for meaning beyond the futility of individual finality, in Arendt's terms – to these tokens of language. What provokes devotion in the reader, within an audience, transforming words – or sounds, gestures, the play of light, images, or sheep – into *signs* or portents is the feeling of wonder. 'It is, precisely, fantasy, imagination, and all their productions, mysteries, fictions, revelations, *all the propensities of the mind to overinterpret God for want of a stable signified of the sacred*'. Such a power of revelation, Malabou notes, follows an economy of 'superstition' whereby 'super' indicates a movement *as if* from 'above' and 'before' – but immanent, *not* external. Etymologically kin to the 'prophetic gifts [of] a seer' (*superstitiosus*) and of 'surviving' (*superstes*) – of persisting beyond (death) – it brings into felt presence something always already existing *potentially*. '*Superstitio* is the gift of second sight which enables a person to know the past as if he or she had been present' (106).

The authority that Goebbels presents us with is not external to the encounter, an augmentation of an origin or foundation carried by tradition – such as a canon – and determined by a curator-priesthood. It involves an immanent dynamic in which audiences might be affected by their power of natality, to bring renewal into being through their capacity for difference and a feeling for wonder that transforms commonplace things into auguries of a meaningful world that endures, that outlasts us. It conjures the desire of the living and the passion for those who have passed on.

Three shining chords gently decay as they diffuse through the space. The music stops.

We placed you in your coffin on Saturday morning, and I supported your head as they carried you. We kissed your cold face for the last time. Then I placed some branches of periwinkle from the garden in the coffin, together with the little portrait of me that you called 'the diligent student', and that you loved.

(*De Materie* libretto)

Marie Curie refuses to let go of her husband. Whilst the discovery of radium emerged from her hypothesis, it could not have been invented without the work they shared, such that the Nobel Prize was 'also an homage to the memory of Pierre Curie'.

The metallic ring of three more chords punctuate her diary entries.

I spend all my time in the laboratory. I do not think that there is anything that I will be able to enjoy apart from perhaps scientific work – and no, not even that. For should I succeed, I could not bear it if you were not aware of it.

Two last chords, the final one heralded by a side-drum roll, and the scene falls into darkness.

6 After Words

Every art has musical principles and when it is completed it becomes itself music. This is even true of philosophy. Friedrich von Schlegel, *Literarische Notizen 1797–1807*. *(Bowie, 2010: 48)*

I have attempted to show with Goebbels and Cage 'that doing something that is not music is music', and with Goehr that the way beyond the work-concept *can* avoid the twinned alternatives of either insisting on its persistence as a transcendental category or disavowing its authority by equalising and standardising it. It can be understood as a feeling for time that is irreducible to but in counterpoint with representation through historical narration. It acts as a mode of producing ways of being in time with others: always differing and ever enduring, 'the continuity of a morphology' in Cage's words. Approached in this way, musicality offers a compositional paradigm through which questions of being – of care – can be addressed immanently, without recourse to an origin, foundation, first cause, or a priori concept.[52]

Curatorial composing involves precisely such a concern for shaping temporal experience in the production of encounters. It does not insist on aesthetic autonomy just as it disturbs individual sovereignty, always inhibiting the

---

[52] I bring being and care into proximity here in part through their articulation by Heidegger in *Being and Time* – itself an important influence on Arendt for whom *The Human Condition* acted as both homage and riposte. Heidegger significantly invoked the fable of Cura, itself an ambivalently 'foundational' myth for the profession of curator (McKeon, 2022a). On musicality more broadly, see Goehr (2008, 2017); Barrett (2016, 2021); and McKeon (2021).

assurance of closure in (self-)identity and the production of insides and out-
sides. In this sense, it manifests through practices that do not make the question
of mediation foundational. Subjects and objects, nature and culture, mind and
body, values and facts, theory and practice, freedom and necessity – these need
not be structuring oppositional terms, requiring the intervention of a third term
or agent to 'balance' or resolve the tensions they articulate. In Goebbels' words,
'the mediation process itself [has] become a theme of art', or if not a theme,
perhaps the *praxis* of an 'absent centre'.

This does not imply the end of *artistic* practice or a diminishment of artists'
work, but it does invite reflection on letting go of authorship and medium
specificity as disciplinary standards. If anything, the turn by many practitioners
in recent decades away from making works for preformed modes of presentation and reception – concerts, exhibitions, theatre, and so on – and towards
staging events, disciplined improvisation, creating new public rituals, collaborative practices, participatory and social aesthetics, is indicative of an impa-
tience with the institutionalisation of the work-concept and its related cultural
norms. Music may no longer have an elementary condition – if it ever did – but
it offers disciplined techniques for putting different elements in motion, in time.

Lastly, my argument suggests a reappraisal may be merited of the relation
between music and spirituality. Often regarded as an embarrassment in modern
times, a regressive refuge or consolation for those unwilling to accept the
disenchantment of the world, music's affinity with a feeling for a 'beyond' if
not a supernatural Other – for the ineffable, as Jankélévich (2003) put it – may
yet provide a means of constructing together a more habitable and durable
world. If authority is not external and fixed but immanent and mutable, always
in the making, it can perhaps be encountered in an effect of being that is
paradoxically both singular – a product of the power of natality in each of us,
the capacity to differ – *and* greater than any individual, the sense of a world that
is bigger than any one of us, more mysterious than words can fathom, and
carried in memory beyond life's span.

References

Adorno, T. W. (1998). *Vers une musique informelle*. In *Quasi una Fantasia: Essays on Modern Music*. Translated by Rodney Livingstone. London: Verso, pp. 269–322.

Adorno, T. W. (1992). Arnold Schoenberg 1874–1951. In *Prisms*. Translated by Samuel Weber and Sherry Weber. Cambridge MA: MIT Press, pp. 149–72.

Althusser, L. (2006). The Underground Current of the Materialism of the Encounter. In *Philosophy of the Encounter: Later Writings, 1978–87*. Translated by G. M. Goshgarian. London: Verso, pp. 163–207.

Arendt, H. (1998). *The Human Condition*. 2nd ed. Chicago, IL: University of Chicago Press.

Arendt, H. (1961). *Between Past and Future: Six Essays in Political Thought*. New York: Viking Press.

Austin, J. L. (1962). *How To Do Things with Words*. Oxford: Clarendon Press.

Austin, L., and Kahn, D., eds. (2011). *Source: Music of the Avant-Garde, 1966–1973*. Berkeley, CA: University of California Press.

Azoulay, A. A. (2019). *Potential History: Unlearning Imperialism*. London: Verso.

Balzer, D. (2015). *Curationism: How Curating Took Over the Art World and Everything Else*. London: Pluto Press.

Barker, J. M. (2010). About 'Songs of Wars I Have Seen'. *The Sunbreak*, 3 March.

Barrett, G. D. (2021). Contemporary Art and the Problem of Music: Towards a Musical Contemporary Art. *Twentieth-Century Music* **18**(2), 223–48. https://doi.org/10.1017/S1478572220000626.

Barrett, G. D. (2016). *After Sound: Toward a Critical Music*. New York: Bloomsbury.

Belford, L. (2020). The Composer as Curator – Following John Cage's Three Compositions for Museum. https://seismograf.org/node/19362 (accessed 6 May 2021).

Benjamin, W. (1998). The Author as Producer. In *Understanding Brecht*. Translated by Anna Bostock. London: Verso, pp. 85–103.

Bernstein, D. W. (2002). John Cage, Arnold Schoenberg, and the Musical Idea. In D. W. Patterson, ed., *John Cage: Music, Philosophy, and Intention, 1933–1950*. New York: Routledge, pp. 15–46.

Bonds, M. E. (2014). *Absolute Music: The History of an Idea*. Oxford: Oxford University Press.

Bonds, M. E. (2006). *Music as Thought: Listening to the Symphony in the Age of Beethoven*. Princeton, NJ: Princeton University Press.

Boulez, P. (1986). *Orientations: Collected Writings*. Edited by Jean-Jacques Nattiez. Translated by Martin Cooper. London: Faber.

Bowie, A. (2010). *Philosophical Variations: Music as 'Philosophical Language'*. Malmö: Northwestern State University Press.

Bowie, A. (2007). *Music, Philosophy, and Modernity*. Cambridge: Cambridge University Press.

Brooks, W. (2002). Music and Society. In D. Nicholls, ed., *The Cambridge Companion to John Cage*. Cambridge: Cambridge University Press, pp. 214–26.

Brown, K. (2002). Visual Art. In D. Nicholls, ed., *The Cambridge Companion to John Cage*. Cambridge: Cambridge University Press, pp. 109–27.

Bürger, P. (1984). *Theory of the Avant-Garde*. Translated by Michael Shaw. Minneapolis, MN: University of Minnesota Press.

Cage, J. (2016). *The Selected Letters of John Cage*. Edited by Laura Kuhn. Middletown, CT: Wesleyan University Press.

Cage, J. (1988). *Anarchy*. Middletown, CT: Wesleyan University Press.

Cage, J. (1983). *X: Writings '79–'82*. Middletown, CT: Wesleyan University Press.

Cage, J. (1981a). *For the Birds: John Cage in Conversation with Daniel Charles*. Boston, MA: Marion Boyars.

Cage, J. (1981b). *Empty Words: Writings '73–'78*. Middletown, CT: Wesleyan University Press.

Cage, J. (1974/1979). The Future of Music. In *Empty Words: Writings '73–'78*. Middletown, CT: Wesleyan University Press, pp. 177–87.

Cage, J. (1973). *M: Writings '67–'72*. London: Marion Boyars.

Cage, J. (1968). *Silence: Lectures and Writings*. London: Marion Boyars.

Cage, J. (1954/1968). 45′ for a Speaker. In *Silence: Lectures and Writings*. London: Marion Boyars, pp. 146–93.

Canetti, E. (1982). *The Torch in My Ear*. Translated by Joachim Neugroschel. London: Granta.

Canetti, E. (1973). *Crowds and Power*. Translated by Carol Stewart. London: Penguin.

Castellucci, R. (2014). Dance is Not the Means, but the Idea. *Le Sacre du Printemps*.Romeo Castellucci. dir. Gebläsehalle, Landschaftspark Duisburg-Nord: Ruhrtriennale. First performance: 15 August 2014.

Cherlin, M. (2000). Dialectical Opposition in Schoenberg's Music and Thought. *Music Theory Spectrum* **22**(2), 157–76.

Christou, J. (1968). Protoperformance. In A. M. Lucciano, ed., *Jani Christou: The Works and Temperament of a Greek Composer*. Amsterdam: Harwood Academic, pp. 146–51.

Coenan, A. (2014). De Materie: Ein musikalischer Essay mit theatralen Illustrationen. *De Materie*. Heiner Goebbels. dir. Kraftzentrale, Landschaftspark Duisburg-Nord: Ruhrtriennale. First performance: 15 August 2014.

Crohn Schmitt, N. (1990). *Actors and Onlookers: Theater and Twentieth-Century Scientific Views of Nature*. Evanston, IL: Northwestern University Press.

Danto, A. (1981). *The Transfiguration of the Commonplace: A Philosophy of Art*. Cambridge, MA: Harvard University Press.

Derrida, J. (2002). The Animal That Therefore I Am (More to Follow). Translated by David Wills. *Critical Inquiry* **28**, 369–418.

Derrida, J. (1987). *The Truth in Painting*. Translated by Geoff Bennington and Ian McLeod. Chicago, IL: University of Chicago Press.

Eisler, H. (1999). *A Rebel in Music*. Edited by Manfred Grabs. London: Kahn & Averill.

Eisler, H. (1975/2014). *Brecht, Music and Culture: Hanns Eisler in Conversation with Hans Bunge*. Edited and translated by Sabine Berendse and Paul Clements. London: Bloomsbury.

Feisst, S. M. (2009). John Cage and Improvisation: An Unresolved Relationship. In G. Solis and B. Nettl, eds., *Musical Improvisation: Art, Education, and Society*. Urbana, IL: University of Illinois Press, pp. 38–51.

Foster, H., ed. (1988). *Vision and Visuality*. Seattle, WA: Bay Press.

Foucault, M. (2009). *Security, Territory, Population: Lectures at the Collège de France 1977–1978*. Edited by Michel Senellart. Translated by Graham Burchell. Basingstoke: Palgrave Macmillan.

Foucault, M. (1998). What Is an Author? In J. D. Faubion, ed., *Aesthetics, Method, and Epistemology*. Translated by James Harkness. New York: The New Press, pp. 205–22.

Gann, K. (2010). *No Such Thing as Silence: John Cage's 4'33"*. New Haven, CT: Yale University Press.

Goebbels, H. (2019). On Aesthetic Experience as Anachronic Experience. In P. de Assis and M. Schwab, eds., *Futures of the Contemporary: Contemporaneity, Untimeliness, and Artistic Research*. Ghent: Orpheus Institute, pp. 85–95.

Goebbels, H. (2018a). There Is No Such Thing as a Giessen School. *Polish Theatre Journal* **1**(5), 1–7.

Goebbels, H. (2018b). Theater als Erfahrung – Die Editorials 2012 / 2013 /2014. In M. Woltas, S. Heppekausen, R. Junicke, and G. Hiß, eds., *Das Theater der Ruhrtriennale: Die ersten sechzehn Jahre*. Oberhausen: Athena Verlag, pp. 266–74.

Goebbels, H. (2017). The Sound of Things. In B. Herzogenrath, ed., *Sonic Thinking: A Mediaphilosophical Approach*. New York: Bloomsbury, pp. 87–97.

Goebbels, H. (2015). *Aesthetics of Absence: Texts on Theatre*. Edited by Jane Collins. Translated by David Roesner and Christina M. Lagao. London: Routledge.

Goebbels, H. (2014). Editorial. In *Ruhrtriennale Festival Brochure*.

Goebbels, H. (2013). Editorial. In *Ruhrtriennale Festival Brochure*.

Goebbels, H. (2012). Editorial. In *Ruhrtriennale Festival Brochure*.

Goebbels, H. (2008). Interview with Andrea Ravagnan, Preparation for an Article in *Il Giornale della Musica*. *Il Giornale della Musica*, November. www.heinergoebbels.com/en/archive/texts/interviews/read/528 (accessed 22 October 2020).

Goebbels, H. (1997/2002). Gegen das Gesamtknstwerk: Zur Differenz der Kunste. In W. Sandner, ed., *Komposition als Inszenierung*. Berlin: Henschel, pp. 135–41.

Goebbels, H. (1996/2002). Musik entziffern: Das Sample als Zeichen. In W. Sandner, ed., *Komposition als Inszenierung*. Berlin: Henschel, pp. 181–5.

Goebbels, H. (1996). 'Opening Up the Text'. *Performance Research Journal* 1:1, 52–58.

Goebbels, H. (1995). More Like an Architect: Interview with Stephan Buchberger. *Theaterschrift* 9. www.heinergoebbels.com/en/archive/texts/interviews/read/91 (accessed 12 August 2022).

Goebbels, H. (1988/2002). Prince and the Revolution: Über das Neue. In W. Sandner, ed., *Komposition als Inszenierung*. Berlin: Henschel, pp. 204–8.

Goebbels, H., and Gourgouris, S. (2004). Performance as Composition: Heiner Goebbels Interviewed by Stathis Gourgouris. *Performing Arts Journal* 26(3), 1–16.

Goehr, L. (2017). 'All Art Constantly Aspires to the Condition of Music' – Except the Art of Music: Reviewing the Contest of the Sister Arts. In P. A. Kottman, ed., *The Insistence of Art: Aesthetic Philosophy after Early Modernity*. New York: Fordham University Press, pp. 140–69.

Goehr, L. (2008). *Elective Affinities: Musical Essays on the History of Aesthetic Theory*. New York: Columbia University Press.

Goehr, L. (2007). *The Imaginary Museum of Musical Works: An Essay in the Philosophy of Music*. Revised ed. Oxford: Oxford University Press.

Green, A. (2018). *When Artists Curate: Contemporary Art and the Exhibition as Medium*. London: Reaktion Books.

Hamilton, J. (2013). *Security: Politics, Humanity, and the Philology of Care*. Princeton, NJ: Princeton University Press.

Hartog, F. (2015). *Regimes of Historicity: Presentism and Experiences of Time.* Translated by Saskia Brown. New York: Columbia University Press.

Heller-Roazen, D. (2011). *The Fifth Hammer: Pythagoras and the Disharmony of the World.* New York: Zone Books.

Hicks, M. (1990). John Cage's Studies with Schoenberg. *American Music* **8**(2), 125–40.

Jackson, S., and Marincola, P., eds. (2020). In Terms of Performance. Produced by Pew Center for Arts & Heritage, Philadelphia and Arts Research Center, University of California, Berkeley. www.intermsofperformance.site (accessed 14 August 2020).

Jameson, F. (2010). *The Hegel Variations: On the Phenomenology of Spirit.* London: Verso.

Jankélévich, V. (2003). *Music and the Ineffable.* Translated by Carolyn Abbate. Princeton, NJ: Princeton University Press.

Jay, M. (2002). Cultural Relativism and the Visual Turn. *Journal of Visual Culture* **1**(3), 267–78.

Jay, M. (1993). *Downcast Eyes: The Denigration of Vision in Twentieth-Century French Thought.* Berkeley, CA: University of California Press.

Karp, I. (1990). Culture and Representation. In I. Karp and S. D. Lavine, eds., *Exhibiting Cultures: The Poetics and Politics of Museum Display.* Washington, DC: Smithsonian Institution, pp. 11–24.

Kass, R. (2001). Diary: Cage's Mountain Lake Workshop, April 8–15, 1990. In D. W. Bernstein and C. Hatch, eds., *Writings through John Cage's Music, Poetry, and Art.* Chicago, IL: University of Chicago Press, pp. 244–59.

Kostelanetz, R., ed. (1988). *Conversing with Cage.* London: Omnibus Press.

Krauss, R. (1993). *The Optical Unconscious.* Cambridge, MA: MIT Press.

Kwon, M. (2002). *One Place after Another: Site-Specific Art and Locational Identity.* Cambridge, MA: MIT Press.

Lehmann, H.-T. (2006). *Postdramatic Theatre.* Translated by Karen Jürs-Munby. London: Routledge.

Lewis, G. (2015). Foreword. In R. L. Packer and M. J. Leach, eds., *Gay Guerilla: Julius Eastman and His Music.* Rochester, NY: University of Rochester Press, pp. vii–xix.

Lewis, G. (2007). Mobilitas Animi: Improvising Technologies, Intending Chance. *Parallax* **13**(4), 108–22.

Mac Low, J. (2001). Cage's Writings up to the Late 1980s. In D. W. Bernstein and C. Hatch, eds., *Writings through John Cage's Music, Poetry, and Art.* Chicago, IL: University of Chicago Press, pp. 210–33.

Malabou, C. (2016). Before and Above: Spinoza and Symbolic Necessity. *Critical Inquiry* **43**, 84–109.

Malabou, C. (2015). The Crowd. Translated by Dashiell Wasserman. *Oxford Literary Review* **37**(1), 25–44.

Malabou, C. (2013). Go Wonder: Subjectivity and Affects in Neurobiological Times. In A. Johnston and C. Malabou, *Self and Emotional Life: Philosophy, Psychoanalysis, and Neuroscience*. New York: Columbia University Press, pp. 3–72.

Malabou, C. (2005). *The Future of Hegel: Plasticity, Temporality and Dialectic*. Translated by Lisabeth During. Preface by Jacques Derrida. Oxford: Routledge.

Malraux, A. (1974). Museum without Walls. In *Voices of Silence*. Translated by Stuart Gilbert. St Albans: Paladin, pp. 13–130.

Martinon, J.-P. (2021). *Curating as Ethics*. Minneapolis, MN: University of Minnesota Press.

Martinon, J.-P., ed. (2013). *The Curatorial: A Philosophy of Curating*. London: Bloomsbury.

Matthews, L. (2019). Heiner Goebbels's *Stifter's Dinge* and the Arendtian Public Sphere. *Performance Philosophy* **5**(1), 109–27.

McKeon, E. (2022a). Cura, the Curatorial, and Paradoxes of Care. *Performance Research Journal* **27**(6–7).

McKeon, E. (2022b). Coming to Our Senses: From the Birth of the Curator Function to Curating Live Arts. *TURBA* **1**(1), 33–52.

McKeon, E. (2021). Making Art Public: Musicality and the Curatorial. Unpublished PhD thesis, Birmingham City University. www.open-access.bcu.ac.uk/13406/ (accessed 12 August 2022).

Mirza, M. (2012). *The Politics of Culture: The Case for Universalism*. Basingstoke: Palgrave Macmillan.

Nattiez, J.-J., ed. (1994). *The Boulez-Cage Correspondence*. Translated by Robert Samuels. Cambridge: Cambridge University Press.

Neff, S. (2014). Point/Counterpoint: John Cage Studies with Arnold Schoenberg. *Contemporary Music Review* **33**(5–6), 451–82.

Obrist, H.-U. O. (2020). Do It. *Independent Curators International*. https://curatorsintl.org/exhibitions/18072-do-it-2013 (accessed 12 August 2022).

Oliveros, P. (1974). *Sonic Meditations*. Baltimore, MD: Smith.

Osborne, P. (2018). *The Postconceptual Condition*. London: Verso.

Parsons Smith, C. (1995). Athena at the Manuscript Club: John Cage and Mary Carr Moore. *Musical Quarterly* **79**(2), 351–67.

Perloff, M. (2012). Difference and Discipline: The Cage/Cunningham Aesthetic Revisited. *Contemporary Music Review* **31**(1), 19–35.

Piekut, B. (2011). *Experimentalism Otherwise: The New York Avant-Garde and Its Limits*. Berkeley, CA: University of California Press.

Piekut, B., ed. (2014). *Tomorrow is the Question: New Directions in Experimental Music Studies*. Ann Arbor, MI: University of Michigan Press.

Pritchett, J. (1993). *The Music of John Cage*. Cambridge: Cambridge University Press.

Ramović, A. (2018). Respecting the Differences, Composing the Distances: Heiner Goebbels' Works as Landscapes with Sonic Paradoxes. In J.-P. Hiekel, ed., *Clash! Generationen – Kulturen – Identitäten in der Gegenwartsmusik*. Mainz: Schott/Darmstadt, pp. 120–42.

Ravenscroft, B. (2006). Re-Construction: Cage and Schoenberg. *Tempo* **60** (235), 2–14.

Rebstock, M., and Roesner, D., eds. (2012). *Composed Theatre: Aesthetics, Practices, Processes*. Bristol: Intellect.

Retallack, J. (1996). *Musicage: Cage Muses on Words, Art, Music*. Hanover, NH: Wesleyan University Press.

Riley, A. (2021). In Pursuit of Non-Knowledge: Perspectives on Performing with the Merce Cunningham Dance Company. Unpublished PhD thesis, De Montfort University. https://dora.dmu.ac.uk/handle/2086/21702 (accessed 26 June 2022).

Rilke, R. M. (2000). *Duino Elegies*. Translated by Edward Snow. New York: North Point Press.

Robinson, H. (2020). Curating Good Participants? Audiences, Democracy and Authority in the Contemporary Museum. *Museum Management and Curatorship* **35**(5), 470–87.

Rockwell, J. (1989). Robert Wilson Stages 'De Materie', a New Opera. *New York Times*, 8 June.

Roesner, D. (2014). *Musicality in Theatre: Music as Model, Method and Metaphor in Theatre-Making*. Farnham: Ashgate.

Ruhrtriennale. (2014). *De Materie* programme.

Schoenberg, A. (1983). *Structural Functions of Harmony*. Edited by Leonard Stein. Translated by Leo Black. London: Faber.

Schoenberg, A. (1975). *Style and Idea: Selected Writings*. Edited by Leonard Stein. Translated by Leo Black. London: Faber.

Schoenberg, A. (1948/1975). A Self Analysis. In L. Stein, ed., *Style and Idea: Selected Writings*. London: Faber, pp. 76–9.

Schoenberg, A. (1938/1975). Teaching and Modern Trends in Music. In L. Stein, ed., *Style and Idea: Selected Writings*. London: Faber, pp. 376–7.

Schoenberg, A. (1931/1975). Linear Counterpoint. In L. Stein, ed., *Style and Idea: Selected Writings*. London: Faber, pp. 289–95.

Silverman, K. (2010). *Begin Again: A Biography of John Cage*. New York: Alfred Knopf.

Steingo, G. (2014). The Musical Work Reconsidered, in Hindsight. *Current Musicology* **97**, 81–112.

Szymczyk, A. (2017). Iterability and Otherness – Learning and Working from Athens. In Q. Latimer and A. Szymczyk, eds., *The documenta 14 Reader*. Kassel: documenta and Museum Fridericianum, pp. 17–42.

Taruskin, R. (2009). No Ear for Music: The Scary Purity of John Cage. In *The Danger of Music: and Other Anti-Utopian Essays*. Berkeley, CA: University of California Press, pp. 261–79.

Tenney, J. (1983/2015). John Cage and the Theory of Harmony. In L. Polansky, L. Pratt, R. Wannamaker, and M. Winter, eds., *From Scratch: Writings in Music Theory*. Urbana, IL: University of Illinois Press, pp. 280–304.

Thorau, C., and Ziemer, H., eds. (2019). *The Oxford Handbook of Music Listening in the 19th and 20th Centuries*. Oxford: Oxford University Press.

Till, N. (2002). Street Fighting Mensch. *The Wire*, November.

Warburton, D., and Livingston, G. (1997). An Interview with Heiner Goebbels. *Paris Transatlantic: Paris New Music Review*, Spring. https://bit.ly/3JOuVdl (accessed 27 October 2020).

World Architecture Community. (2016). IBA Emscher Park, Germany. https://vimeo.com/146888523 (accessed 19 October 2020).

Acknowledgements

This Element addresses the question of authority so it would be remiss of me to let the issue of my own authorship pass without comment. This is the work of many people for which I take responsibility, not least for any errors or misjudgements. It follows my doctoral research on musicality and the curatorial, which benefited enormously from the guidance of my supervisors Nick Gebhardt, Johnny Golding, and Tim Wall, and from engaged discussion with John Mowitt. I have had the great pleasure to share and discuss aspects of this with friends, colleagues, and well-wishers, including Mavis McKeon, Andy Ingamells, Robert Fink, Mirjam Zegers, Matthew Shlomowitz, Christopher Dingle, and Laura Kuhn, whilst my journey of getting to know Heiner Goebbels' work was aided by Hilke and Matthias Wagner, Joe Cutler, Michael Wolters, Chris Cutler, and Kersten Glandien, amongst others. I am especially grateful to Heiner for the interview and exchanges we shared as well as for the images from his productions and permission to reproduce them here. The John Cage Trust has also been generous in providing images with permission, and Wesleyan University Press for the right to use one of Cage's mesostics. David Beard nudged me to seek publication and the series editor Mervyn Cooke has steered the process with consummate professionalism and good spirit. It is dedicated to Annabel, Olivia, and Alexander.

As the foregoing Element suggests, the question of authority lies here, at the text's end, in its proper place with your reading of it. It is neither my property nor yours, neither in the 'text itself' nor outside it. If authority is to be encountered it will be in their points of contact, waiting patiently in the dream light of dusk for the arrival of dawn.

Cambridge Elements ⹀

Music Since 1945

Mervyn Cooke

University of Nottingham

Mervyn Cooke brings to the role of series editor an unusually broad range of expertise, having published widely in the fields of twentieth-century opera, concert and theatre music, jazz, and film music. He has edited and co-edited *Cambridge Companions to Britten, Jazz, Twentieth-Century Opera*, and *Film Music*. His other books include *Britten: War Requiem, Britten and the Far East, A History of Film Music, The Hollywood Film Music Reader, Pat Metheny: The ECM Years*, and two illustrated histories of jazz. He is currently co-editing (with Christopher R. Wilson) *The Oxford Handbook of Shakespeare and Music*.

About the Series

Elements in Music Since 1945 is a highly stimulating collection of authoritative online essays that reflects the latest research into a wide range of musical topics of international significance since the Second World War. Individual Elements are organised into constantly evolving clusters devoted to such topics as art music, jazz, music and image, stage and screen genres, music and media, music and place, immersive music, music and movement, music and politics, music and conflict, and music and society. The latest research questions in theory, criticism, musicology, composition and performance are also given cutting-edge and thought-provoking coverage. The digital-first format allows authors to respond rapidly to new research trends, with contributions being updated to reflect the latest thinking in their fields, and the essays are enhanced by the provision of an exciting range of online resources.

Cambridge Elements ≡

Music Since 1945

CPSIA information can be obtained
at www.ICGtesting.com
Printed in the USA
LVHW080118231122
733856LV00016B/1271

9 781009 337601